The *Beautiful* Call

When God Reveals Our Name

———◦◦———

GodSpeak - Book I

BRIAN LOUIS PERKINS

The Beautiful Call: When God Reveals Our Name

Brian Louis Perkins

The Beautiful Call: When God Reveals Our Name

The Beautiful Call: When God Reveals Our Name (GodSpeak, Book 1) Copyright © 2020 by Brian Louis Perkins

All rights reserved. No part of this publication may be reproduced, distributed or transmitted in any form or by any means, including photocopying, recording, or other electronic or mechanical methods, without the prior written permission of the publisher, except in the case of brief quotations embodied in critical reviews and certain other noncommercial uses permitted by copyright law. For permission requests, write to the author via the email below.

Scripture is taken from the New King James Version®. Copyright © 1982 by Thomas Nelson. Used by permission. All rights reserved.

Scriptures marked KJV are taken from the KING JAMES VERSION (KJV): KING JAMES VERSION, public domain.

Scripture quotations marked (NIV) are taken from the Holy Bible, New International Version®, NIV®. Copyright © 1973, 1978, 1984, 2011 by Biblica, Inc.™ Used by permission of Zondervan. All rights reserved worldwide. www.zondervan.com The "NIV" and "New International

Version" are trademarks registered in the United States Patent and Trademark Office by Biblica, Inc.™

Scripture marked ISV was taken from the Holy Bible: International Standard Version®. Copyright © 1996-forever by The ISV Foundation. ALL RIGHTS RESERVED INTERNATIONALLY. Used by permission.

Scripture quotations marked ESV are from the ESV® Bible (The Holy Bible, English Standard Version®), copyright © 2001 by Crossway, a publishing ministry of Good News Publishers. Used by permission. All rights reserved.

Scripture quotations marked MSG are taken from THE MESSAGE, copyright © 1993, 2002, 2018 by Eugene H. Peterson. Used by permission of NavPress. All rights reserved. Represented by Tyndale House Publishers, a Division of Tyndale House Ministries. Scripture quotations marked NASB taken from the New American Standard Bible® (NASB), Copyright © 1960, 1962, 1963, 1968, 1971, 1972, 1973, 1975, 1977, 1995 by The Lockman Foundation. Used by permission. www.Lockman.org

Scripture quotations marked JUB (or JBS) are taken from the Jubilee Bible (or Biblia del Jubileo), copyright ©

2000, 2001, 2010, 2013 by Russell M. Stendal. Used by permission of Russell M. Stendal, Bogota, Colombia. All rights reserved.

Scripture quotations marked KJV2000 are taken from The King James 2000 Bible, copyright © Doctor of Theology Robert A. Couric 2000, 2003, Used by permission. All rights reserved.

Some Scripture has been bolded or italicized for emphasis by the author.

The Beautiful Call: When God Reveals Our Name (GodSpeak, Book 1)/Brian Louis Perkins ISBN 978-1-7348754-1-6

Brian Louis Perkins

One crowded hour of glorious life
Is worth an age without a name.

"The Call" by Thomas Osbert Mordaunt

The Beautiful Call: When God Reveals Our Name

CONTENTS

CONTENTS	9
DEDICATION	10
THE WAYWARD CALL	**11**
THE FIRST CALL - IDENTITY	**21**
1 IDENTITY THEFT	23
2 WHAT'S IN A NAME	29
3 NAME ABOVE ALL NAMES	46
4 WHEN GOD CALLS OUR NAME	55
5 THE BEAUTIFUL CALL	70
THE SECOND CALL - DESTINY	**100**
6 THE NAME-CALLER	113
7 OUR SECOND NAME	125
8 STUCK BETWEEN TWO NAMES	131
9 NAMES MEAN SOMETHING IN THE SPIRITUAL	139
10 GOD WILL MAKE OUR NAME GREAT	160
THE THIRD CALL - TIME	**168**
11 THE BEAUTIFUL GATE	172
12 THE UNPREDICTABLE NOW	182
13 CALLING OUR FUTURE AND PAST INTO OUR NOW	198
THE FINAL CALL - REVELATION	**228**
14 CALL OF THE BEAUTIFIER	230
15 THE BIG REVEAL OF US	250
16 THE MOST VALUABLE IN THE WORLD	264
17 THE BIG REVEAL	278
18 IF YOU HEAR MY VOICE:	292
ENDNOTES	**298**
ABOUT THE AUTHOR	307
CONTACT	315

DEDICATION

To the Man who whispered my name from heaven and showed me what was behind the tree where God speaks.

Brian Louis Perkins

The Wayward Call

> *Like a bird that wanders from its nest is a man who wanders from his place.*
>
> - Proverbs 27:8

GOD TEACHES US FROM NATURE, using things we already see to explain Himself to us. From things that we are familiar with He reveals those things about Himself which are unfamiliar. Often, the Lord uses birds, and out of Scripture we can see this for we all know about the teachings concerning sparrows, eagles, and of course, doves. In fact, so frequently are birds employed in this manner that Job was moved to write:

> *ask... the birds of the air, and they will tell you.*
>
> - Job 12:7

Recently, He used some local birds to show something most of us gloss over in our own lives. These birds were not sparrows, eagles, or doves, but peacocks, instead.

Near a certain house there is a preserve with lots of trees and a small river running through it. The home borders a wilderness area where exotic creatures stroll down the street as common entertainment. Raccoons, squirrels, garden-variety snakes, cottontail rabbits, foxes, bobcats, and the infamous alligator are all in the area making appearances at one time or another.

Animals abound everywhere.

The rarest of them all is the *pavo cristatus*, more famously known as the peacock, which also lives in the preserve. Since they are not native to the area, they are most unusual and the most beautiful. Liberated into the wild, someone's pets grew into several peacock families that surprisingly rule the neighborhoods with impunity.

Roosting in trees, roofs of houses, or sometimes cars, they are found often casually walking down the middle of streets as if they own them. Carrying a bit of attitude, they exhibit real sense of superiority since they know they are glorious to look at and strut their way to prominence. If they lived in Hollywood, they would own the runway.

These families have babies year after year, as mothers walk down the streets and into yards with their newborn, allowing their chicks to experience the world around them, but if needed, the fledglings find a protective shelter huddling under their mother's wings. If they venture too close to people, there is a certain cluck a mother will use to signify danger that frantically pulls the children underfoot. No army has a more efficient regiment for they know their mother has a call to safety.

Most people do not realize how loud peacocks are. They make lots of noise, and they make it all the time. There are honks, clucks, whirs, and something like a foghorn.

The patriarch with his glorious tail feathers revealed a uniquely beautiful call made for a certain 98-year-old neighbor. It was a longer musical vocalization reserved only for her. Displaying his feathers, he does the "peacock dance" at her front door nearly every day during the season so she can come out with her cane to watch. The two must have been friends a long time.

Another time, a scene presented itself where a young peacock, who had just learned of its ability to fly, had perched himself a little too high in the nearby woods. This youngster stranded himself in the upper branches, too afraid to come down on his own. Because of where he was, fear controlled him. He frantically called out to his mother.

Baby peacocks make a sound like a "whir" when they feel at ease, but this young bird was not whirring; he was on the edge of terror. No interpreter was needed to understand the call for help, and the whole neighborhood heard it.

Not too far away, his mother approached in the street worrying about her little one the way only mothers can do. She stood with her other chicks on the ground, incessantly honked, calling to her wayward child who had put himself into danger. The scene grew tense as the mother's calls became more frantic. Tension was in the air.

Her communication could be understood with those sounds, "Come home, my son. Follow my voice, and I will guide you out of this scary situation."

Peahens have been taking care of their young since the beginning of creation, but the drama was real; it was literally "in the air." How could this little bird get into such a predicament?

Yet, God opened a door of understanding through this moment of chaos. He was illustrating the beautiful call of a mother's voice, who would make everything turn out all right if only the young child would obey her directions.

The Lord was speaking here.

This was a shadow of a human drama played out in nature, having a lesson teaching in a sort of living theater. Have we not found ourselves in this predicament at one time or the other, or maybe we are in the thick of it now? Through the peacock, we saw that all we need to do during our time of greatest peril; we simply needed to discover where God was speaking. If we hear and obey His voice, He will show us a way to safety.

No one can miss the tone of a parent's heart-breaking cry who is trying to bring home their wandering child, and aren't we all a little like that daring peacock stuck in a tree crying for help? We have tried to show the world how capable we are with our abilities, but we end up in a desperate situation in need of drastic aid. Even then, during our mess, the Lord speaks, telling us to follow His voice, knowing that if we listen to Him, everything will turn out all right.

The voice of God is beautiful.

He shows us in nature by a mother's call how much He is trying to get us to listen to His instructions so we can safely come home. Even more so, the Lord is calling us with personal encounters and spiritual words, which we can barely describe.

And a voice came out of heaven.

Mark 1:11

There is something we all want to know. The questions each of us ask are: "Does God still speak today" and, "Will He talk to us directly?"

The resounding answer is, "Yes!" In this book, we will discover that He communicates twenty-four hours a day, seven days a week, and from the beginning of the world to its end. In fact, there is rarely a time when He is not speaking.

The Beautiful Call: When God Reveals Our Name

The Lord spoke at the beginning of Creation, and His voice is still ringing out that today is our opportunity to hear from heaven. Nature also has a sound that is speaking, just like the One who created it, pouring forth speech every minute of every day.

God's voice is available for us, but we must catch its sound.

Consider when a voice spoke from the sky as Jesus walked on the earth. We observe the scene as written in the Gospel of John, where the Son of God began to predict His death on the cross. The lord begins, "Father, glorify Your name," to which the sky opens to respond. The voice of God blared throughout the atmosphere for all to hear.

> *Then a voice came from heaven, saying, "I have both glorified it and will glorify it again." Therefore, the people who stood by and **heard it** said that **it had thundered**. Others said, "An angel **has spoken** to Him."*
>
> John 12:28-29, emphasis added

When God speaks from the spiritual realm, three kinds of people are always around to witness it.

There are those who hear only physical noises – "some said it thundered" - because they cannot believe beyond what their five senses reveal to them. Then there are others who said it was indeed a spiritual thing, but it was something other than the Lord – "some said it was an angel." Finally, there is the third kind who hears God speak from heaven.

When the Lord's voice rumbles, we can have one of these three responses to what He says: we can perceive it correctly, listen in error, or detect nothing at all. But if we expect to hear Him then there is more significance in it than we can imagine. This book can become a fantastic interaction with the Lord if we hear Him speak to us as we read. If we have ears to listen to what God is saying, then we find He delivers a fresh understanding of world-shaking events.

When God speaks, everything aligns

The Beautiful Call: When God Reveals Our Name

To be sure, the voice of the Lord is almost mystical when we initially catch it since it is full of wonder. In our experience, it is as if we have discovered some mystery no one else as ever known and we ask ourselves, "Did we just unearth some hidden secret?" There is a deep mystery in hearing Him for the first time.

He does not speak once, and that is all, no. He talks frequently, connecting with our now. While we drive our cars, wash our clothes, or mow our lawns, the Lord desires to speak. But be aware, once begun, He opens like a floodgate, and His words flow out constantly.

Since people can hear God's voice in three different ways, He makes three different calls to mankind, and then a fourth. May we long to discover the Lord's beautiful call, because the Father is giving us His "call" for us to walk with Him in a safe place.

The First Call - Identity

Brian Louis Perkins

1
Identity Theft

> *The thief does not come except to steal... I have come that they may have life...*
>
> -John 10:10

Danger, danger, danger.

We hear it all the time: "Woman falls prey to identity theft," or "Couple targeted, identity stolen." It happens when least expected and is always inconvenient. When this happens to us, we think we know who we are, but the world does not recognize us as our true selves, and we become entangled with an identity crisis that can last for years. After a while, though, things begin to blur around our life status and who we were supposed to be. Now, after becoming tired of fighting to remember, we forget about our uniqueness, submitting to a slow fade into a group mentality. We lose ourselves within the masses and are no longer a distinct individual.

We become a mess when we do not know who we are. Look at this world and its disorder, and we witness a society suffering from an identity crisis.

Most of us walking on this planet are victims of identity theft, yet we do not realize what has happened. Everything for us has become grey. We were robbed and wander around like orphans from the movie Oliver. We are like those lost children in Peter Pan, or worse yet, we have formed into a corrupted society similar to those abandoned lads in the Lord of the Flies.

The problem is simple: someone removed all our identification markers at birth, so no trace of our beginning remains. Deep down, we understand something is not right. We have become an amnesia culture that rambles about, not remembering our name, what family we belong to, or who our Father is.

A voice flutters in the back of our mind that there is a big secret about us, compelling us to seek out what that missing information is. Unsettled in our place and timing, never fitting in anywhere, we aimlessly roam from one group to another, going from thrill to thrill because inside, we feel the need to realign our station in life. "Don't stay here; this is not the right place for you," we hear a voice whisper. "Go, find out who you are."

Acknowledging this is right, but also realizing that we need help to get where we should go, we wander and roam. If only someone remembered our original name, we might re-establish our true self. However, as we ask around, we only gather half-truths, unfulfilling answers, or outright lies about our worth.

Can we find anyone who can give us a clue about who we really are?

There is only One person who remembers who we are, and His name is the Heavenly Father. If we catch His beautiful call, then He will not only inform us of our identity, but He will reveal that we are supposed to belong to a wealthy family with a famous name. We are the missing children of the Father's house for whom He sent His Son to make way for lost souls to come home.

We need to understand that God has a magnificent name. It takes Someone with a name that is great to call us into greatness. It takes Someone with a great name to call us to our place. Excellence has to be found in one person for it to spread to others, and God said He would make our name great in all the earth. We become well known because we discover we belong to a well-known family with a great name.

When we distinguish that God is whispering our earthly name, a fantastic transfer will occur, and we are instantly changed. He calls the name we were born with, so we can be born again. The Lord calls our name in the physical, so we will lift our eyes to glimpse at the spiritual for the first time. When He calls us on the earth, He wants to show us heaven, which is something more significant.

God knows us personally, and when He calls our earthly name, He reveals our identity to us. It tells us who we are, moves us into our proper occupance, and begins to rewrite our lost ways for we are now found.

Finally, when the One who created the heavens speaks our name, we will engage in an encounter we will never forget. Not only do we realize we belong somewhere, but we discover the search for us has been going on for a long time.

As light shines in our darkness, we immediately know who we are because God calls our name. Names connect and bring change. We link to the name He reveals to us, and it will change the course of our entire life.

So, what is in a name?

2
What's In A Name

A good name is to be chosen rather than great riches...

Proverbs 22:1

Names are powerful.

The Bible tells us a good name is better to have than wealth because an excellent name brings a certain prestige bearing honor. We think about someone differently who has created a successful business out of nothing, making their way to the top compared to someone who has cheated and stolen their way into the upper ranks. Though both have money, one earned theirs while the other did not, and to a hard worker, we assign honor while we withhold it from a thief. Mentioned in the same sentence, we never come to similar conclusions about the two of them. Their difference is not in their financial strength but in their name, and as Scripture declares, it is better to obtain an excellent name than to have riches.

A suitable name apart from money is preferable to an awful name with wealth; however, it is superior when an exceptional name holds assets instead of a person with a shady status. It serves to illustrate how names mean something in the earth.

Some people are renowned throughout history for either righteous acts or infamous deeds, while others establish themselves by their riches, power, or fame; we call this a reputation.

A quality name speaks to this status.

A suitable name will serve us well all the days of our life, but if we have a notorious name, it will haunt us to the grave. Herein lies the potential names carry in our world. They open doors, bringing in opportunities for some, but they also close them, leaving others out in the street.

Today, corporations pay a lot of money to become a trusted name in the industry. To earn an excellent reputation with its valuable service or product lines becomes a company's primary goal. Still, critical reviews can turn adored businesses into those passionately hated overnight through one unfortunate misstep. Search engines populate quickly if the brand name turns to dirt, starting a destructive cycle of bad press, which produces a terrible name.

Due to the growing threat against an exceptional name, a new industry has emerged, called "Reputation Management," where a business suffering in such a manner can hire a professional whose sole responsibility is to rescue brand names from negative onslaughts. Companies pay a lot of money to protect a valuable name.

We can trust something with a good reputation because through thick and thin, it gives comfort when needed most. We know love has a superb name throughout all cultures because it is honored everywhere. If we do something in the name of love, people understand because love speaks on a different level that we grasp easily, which brings a particular communication of its actions.

When Jesus came into this world to save humanity, the cross declares the love He offered since He gave His life for His friends. This action was a message understood by all because it holds a great name.

Before detainment, an informed soldier knows if captured in warfare, he can only reveal his name, rank, and serial number. Anyone questioning him from the other side will understand his identification, post, and authorization. By doing this, they tell the enemy, "All you need to know is my name, and by what authority I do what I do." It is expert advice because he uses the reputation of his national army in an opposing situation.

Names carry identification and authority

If we say we are a believer in Jesus Christ, we are using a divine connection bearing the legal clout contained in the name of the Son of God.

And Jesus came and spoke to them, saying, "All authority has been given to Me in heaven and on earth."

Matthew 28:17-19. Emphasis mine.

The Beautiful Call: When God Reveals Our Name

God designed our name to bare the genuine nature of who we are in this world. One of the most comforting things is the power of the family name.

Parents bestow given names upon their children when they are born, which are also called birth names. This title will encompass us our entire life.

We might name a child after a father. His dad may be "James" and could call the son, "Jim," or a daughter, "Jamie." Maybe a child is named for a favored mother, grandmother, or aunt. They called my father after his uncle, while my parents named me after a famous actor. These designations reflect the sentiment of the name-giver, attaching warmth upon the one who will bear it next.

Some people resist the names we call them and will only answer to the name of their choice. A man named John may not like being dubbed "Johnnie" or "John-boy" and will only respond to the name of John. To this man, names mean something.

Throughout human history, when a woman marries a man, she will take on his last name. There are exceptions to this. Whenever a woman changes her name during a marriage, a man is saying to her, "I will give you my name," or toward the man, the wife-to-be is saying, "I will take your name." Through marriage, under her new name, the bride will become part of the family line, with all of its benefits.

Sometimes there is a formal name where the first and last are spoken together, and there are occasions where a person is hailed by their last name. "Hey, Williams, hurry up! Double time!" However, when granted, being on a first-name basis is most rewarding because this infers a level of intimacy between the two who agreed to enter such a privilege.

Names bear identity

We commend a person who has made a name for themselves, as recognition comes from the work they produce, and through their labor, their name brings notoriety.

Then they said, "Come on! Let's... make a name for ourselves..."

Genesis 11:4

They may produce a brand or trade name. When someone hears the name of an individual business, they immediately recognize if it represents a car, a cell phone, or a store.

As a person's work becomes successful, we say they are the big names in their field. If they work hard to become number one, and everyone knows how much effort is required to reach the top, we will say to them, "Hard work is the name of the game."

Once a person or their work has gone "big," we say they have become a household name, one with which everyone is familiar. We will remark about a famous person, "Their name rings a bell." We may want to associate with them or at least to give the impression of such so we may drop names or name names.

If someone wants something, like a food item, for example, they might say, "That donut has my name on it."

Nicknames are usually not the birth names our parents chose for us, but ones which we or close friends (even enemies) assign. Similarly, in the cyber world, we have a screen name or an "avatar," which is a form of a nickname. An actor may have a stage name, an author, a pen name, and a singer may have a professional title. In the days of CB Radios, every user had a "handle," a forerunner of the screen name. Spies may have an alter ego, while military operators have a code name, and criminals several identities called aliases.

When we give a list of choices, we often say, "there is this one or that to choose from, just to name a few." Names in this scenario speak of more than one and are connectors to something bigger, more plentiful than itself.

When we call something, we reveal its genuine nature as God does when He calls our name. These labels are weighty and substantial associations for both earthly and heavenly resources.

When a name becomes a verb instead of a noun, everything changes. Names can connect with unlimited resources.

Consider when we use naming in this manner: "What do you want? Name it, and it is yours." Here "name" becomes a verb, a word of action, and we can name what we want. When we use this phrase in our culture, we intend to say that whatever a person would "name" could be theirs by promise.

Here is another way in which we use "name" as a link to limitless assets. We have heard people say, "When do you want your wedding to happen? Just name the day," or "When do you want the check to hit your bank? Just name the day." It creates an open opportunity to control the timing of an event, picking any day we desire to cause something to happen. "When do you want me to come to visit you? Just name the day." These are examples of an open calendar and great choices put into our hands by making name an action word.

Another way a name becomes a dynamic tool is when something or someone is asked for by name. "The governor has asked for you by name to appear before him." It can also be used in a product sense, "Ask for [this product] or [that product] by name." It is a specific calling, and not just any will do, only the precise thing or person requested. Therefore, when God calls our name, He is asking for us directly, and not anyone else, for only we will do in that situation.

As we focus more on God here, think about the following associations. We baptize in the name of the Father, the Son, and the Holy Ghost. We say, "in heaven's name," or "in the name of God," as common phrases. The Lord openly tells us we are to ask in His name.

And whatever you ask in My name, that I will do, that the Father may be glorified in the Son.

John 14:13, emphasis added

Let us consider the most sobering use of the word "name": Reputation.

We have an awful name, or a name dragged in the mud with sin. We are stained, dirty, and unrighteous, and of ourselves, our name is terrible. Poor life choices and human birth status deny us from reaching our greatest achievements because we are stopped in the name of the Law of Holiness. Sin binds us to the punishment of that Law because we are not in the right.

We may look righteous as we try to wash ourselves and dress well. We attempt to secure higher-paying jobs, attend a magnificent church or country club. Our possessions are what we think will deliver the right name for us when we obtain a better boat, automobile, or home. We envision that they speak on our behalf, yet they do this "in name only," or superficially. This phrase means that even though the name is there, the substance is not, and no reality exists to support the claim. Our name in and of itself is not noble, but we need one of renown since ours usually does not allow us to enter certain places.

When our money is forcibly removed from our possession, we know a thief has done it, and we say they stole our identity. It is similar to psychology's concept of personality disorders. Our soul gets buffeted to the point that we give access to the "voices in our heads." Bullying spirits push our personality to the back burner, so to speak, as they move to the forward position, and we suffer identity theft.

When something hijacks our individualities, we are at risk of being overtaken by a taskmaster who rules this world with an iron fist. We become confused about why we are here and who we are. Assigning his henchmen to bewilder and confuse us, we cannot identify our uniqueness, causing our personalities to become slaves under oppressive spirits. Sadly, we lose our true selves in the masquerade of fitting into the world system, trying to become something never intended.

Experts advise us to be ourselves, yet we habitually give control away in the name of being like everyone else. The strange thing is we do not wish to become what we see ourselves morphing into; we feel it is wrong, and when it savages our mind, we give up our authority. If we forfeit our acceptable name, the devil desires to move in and steal our God-given right of being a particular bearer of heaven's great news.

And there is a price to pay for losing our self to the love of the world. Because of this, we become sinners by name, and as such, are put on trial for a heinous crime whose penalty is a death sentence. Who will fight for us in this onslaught? We have no rights, no one will help those who have fallen, and in desperation, we hang our heads. We have lost who we are supposed to be by making poor choices. Crying out, we ask, "Can anyone clear our name? Can anyone restore our good name?"

However, it is better if the Lord gives us a new worthy name.

We say, "I will stake my reputation on it," meaning we guarantee the result. If we say this it is because we are so sure of the conclusion, whether based upon expertise or experience, that we have risked our good name on the outcome. We risk our name that everything will turn out as we say.

If we can do this as mere mortals, then how much more can God do the same and even more gloriously? He has staked His excellent name on our outcome. What a tremendous statement this is, understanding how often we fail. Who would stake their magnificent name on our result? God did. Not only did He do it, but He also gave the life of His Son as a guarantee. By offering Jesus as a sacrificial Lamb, we can become the sons and daughters of God.

By doing this, we have been allowed to become the person of prestige that we have always dreamed of becoming. This is how we will turn out. We will win, and we will end up with a great name, one that the Father has staked His reputation on - with the life of His Son. It is an incredibly high mark to reach, yet, rest assured, we will.

Created for something better than blending into this world, God wants us to be a standout product of heaven.

There is terrific news for our restoration. By the mercies of God, He will come to us in our dilemma even when others have cast us away, leaving us abandoned along the highway of life. Through this godly action, we will experience the kind of hope that can overtake the hold of a darkness which has kept us imprisoned. Hopelessness breaks apart when heaven's light pours in, extinguishing the lies of the devil until all that remains is a bright future.

When Jesus calls our name, it will alter the course of our entire life, and in responding to His beautiful call, He will take our unsuitable name, cast it as far as the east is from the west, and restore to us one of honor which holds renown. He has done this for others; He will do it for any of us who ask. We only need to hear Him call our name.

> *Ask, and it will be given to you; seek, and you will find; knock, and it will be opened to you.*

The Beautiful Call: When God Reveals Our Name

Matthew 7:7

A little-known fact in Scripture is that every proper name listed, whether person or place, is fused with meaning, and if we study the Hebrew or Greek languages, we see this is so. Every term is utilized with purpose, indicating position, authority, or calling. Anytime we notice the word "name" in the Bible, it points to the dynamic power of relationship.

Ultimately, names are relational. Therefore, take care to answer when God calls our name; it requires a personal response, for the right name to secure our destinies is at hand.

So, what effect can a name have?

Literally, everything.

Brian Louis Perkins

3
Name Above All Names

Therefore, God also has highly exalted Him and given Him the name which is above every name.

Philippians 2:9

God has a great name.

There is a God whose name is more than worthy. His name is everything from Almighty to Resurrection to Wonderful Counselor, and the Bible often recites this cry from those who worship Him: "Who is like Him?"

To be led to greatness, we need to be called by the magnificent One. To be escorted into our future, we need Someone who has journeyed in our past and stands with us in our present as well. The Caller will qualify the called.

When Moses conversed with the Presence emanating out of the burning bush, he said,

> ...*When I come to the children of Israel... and they say to me, 'What is His name?' what shall I say to them?"*
>
> Exodus 3:13

Moses was asking God what His name was, and the Lord answered Him with the following reply.

> *And God said to Moses, "I AM WHO I AM." And He said, "Thus you shall say to the children of Israel, 'I AM has sent me to you.' "*
>
> Exodus 3:14

God's name is not something from a bygone era, "I was," or a time to come, "I will be"; no, His name is in the eternal now, so He calls His name, "I AM." God always is, so He can always be called, "I AM." It is eternity's point of view: He can see history and destiny along with the "now" all at once. This perspective means that all of Time is laid bare before Him, and He is "I AM" at all times, therefore it is natural to call Him in this tense.

He is a God that exists, not existed, nor will exist one day; He is the "I AM" right now.

> *"This is what the Lord says, he who made the earth, the Lord who formed it and established it - the Lord is his name.*
>
> Jeremiah 33:2 NIV

The term "name" appears 864 times in Scripture, which is a figure uniquely associated with Creation. God used His prominent name, the Word, or Beresheet, to establish and frame the worlds, and in them, He utilized the number 864 quite often. These numerals are found throughout the Universe and happen to be the exact amount of appearances the term shem (name) are placed in Scripture.

So, whether in the heaven around us or in Scripture itself, 864 is connected. His name is majestic, and this is why the Hebrew tradition only refers to God as HaShem or The

Name. Eight-hundred sixty-four times, it ties itself to "names" and to Creation.

Here are some examples.

There are 24 hours in one day, 60 minutes in each hour, and 60 seconds in every minute. If we count the day by seconds instead of hours, there are 86,400 seconds in every day. This is 60 x 60 x 12 = 86,400. Do we see the 864 in there?

Therefore, *HaShem*, The Name, or Jesus, controls time for He has left his mark upon it.

We find that the Sun is 864,000 miles in diameter. The shadow the earth casts in space is also 864,000 miles in length. This large numeric was used by the ancient Greek astronomers to establish how far away the moon was from the earth. So, this 864 number helps us discover our place in creation.

Eight-hundred sixty-four is a foundational number, and when applied by Wisdom, it "founded" many things in Creation.

> **"The Lord possessed me [wisdom] at the beginning** of His way, before His works of old. I

have been established from everlasting, from the beginning, before there was ever an earth...

- Psalm 8:22-23, emphasis added

When He prepared the heavens, I was there...
When He marked out the foundations of the earth, **then I was beside Him as a master craftsman**...

- Psalm 8:22-23,27,29-30, emphasis added

The moon's diameter is 2160 miles, and if we divide its breadth by 10, we get 216.0. Taking this, we find something incredible: 216.0*4 = 864. This number reveals 864 is set in the establishment of the moon as well.

Where the Sun is 93 million miles from the earth, it is also foundationally locked by 864. If we use the full distance of 93,312,000, then the following holds true: if we divide that number by 1080, then we get 86,400, the exact number of seconds in a single day, and 864 is there.

God "founded" everything about life on earth through this number.

So, if God uses "name" in Scripture 864 times, He is trying to tell us that names are foundational. They "found" our identity.

His name is above every name, and He wants to tell us His name, personally.

For a period spanning twenty years, I have written and directed a long-running Easter play. This theatrical event is based on the Passion week of Christ, from the Garden of Gethsemane to the Resurrection at the tomb, as most church dramas commonly do during that time of year. Ours, however, does something a little different. For each part, we precede them with a narration about an aspect of God's name. During each section, we utilize a distinct title of God, so that the last sentence of every narrative reads, "His name is [insert name here]."

This last line also describes the action appearing in the upcoming scene; after all, the play is called Name Above All Names.

Some examples of this include: His name is the Lamb of God, or His name is the Resurrection and the Life, His name is the King of Kings, His name is the I AM, etc.

One of the crescendos of the production is a video where the viewer flies through the names of God set to dynamic music, and this has historically produced awe-inspiring moments for the audience.

Everyone gets excited when God draws back the curtain to reveal His name openly. We see evidence of this every year when at the end of our production, we scroll through them on the screen, and the reaction to His great name is always the same: Rousing applause.

Understand that it takes a great name to unveil others' great names, and this is now what He desires to do with us:

The Beautiful Call: When God Reveals Our Name

God wants to tell us who we are, what family we belong to, and who our Father is. He intends to reveal our name with His voice.

4
When God Calls Our Name

"I have called you by your name; you are Mine."

– Isaiah 43:1

We remember when it happened.

God called our name. It seemed as if the Lord stepped down from heaven to meet us face to face. The moment we heard the heavenly voice, new possibilities opened up for us, and the things we thought could not be true, displayed themselves as real the instant we received Jesus into our hearts. We had a divine appointment to meet with the Creator of heaven and earth, and time itself appeared to stop when the Eternal One stepped into our world to whisper our name.

Mary went to the tomb looking for the body of Jesus on the third day after His crucifixion. Though He had already risen from the dead, she could only focus on the rolled-away stone. That huge seal carved out of rock left an emptiness inside of her heart because now the body of Jesus was missing.

Motion jolted her out of deep thought as a man appeared in her line of sight. He was someone she thought of as a gardener, and asked him, "Sir, tell me, where have you taken His body."

In her emotional state, she could not recognize that this Man was not the one who gardened the grounds of this tomb, but instead, was the One who made the grounds of the Garden of Eden. It was Jesus, risen from the dead.

She waited for an answer, unable to identify the silent One standing before her. It was not until the Lord softly spoke her name, "Mary..." that she finally knew who this Gardner was.

Likewise, though we did not perceive the Lord, who is standing so near to us, we will see Him for the first time when He calls our name. Upon the revelation that His voice brings, we will know who it is speaking to us.

The Beautiful Call: When God Reveals Our Name

In Hebrew, the word for "called" is qara, which means "to be named, called out, or chosen."1 The root of this word comes from the idea of a personal encounter, to meet unexpectedly, or to cause to happen.2 This call is private, one arranged by God Himself. He will choose a name for us befitting the gift of eternal life, for it is the salvation moment. There is a specific time God prepares to meet us face to face, changing our lives forever. After this appointment, a shifting occurs as we answer God's call.

For many, this is when we realize God is no longer a myth or fictional character, but a living person, that we are encountering. This breath-taking moment is eminently holy, as the heavens are torn open, and the Lord comes down to personally introduce Himself. It is an instance where nothing else matters, except this meeting, and it suddenly dawns on us for the first time that Jesus is real after all.

But what happens here, precisely? Let us unpack this a bit since, through our modern society, we may have become disassociated with holy things. Terms like "salvation" carry little weight in a world where ethical shifts occur like pendulum swings, where what is righteous one moment becomes evil the next. We become confused by relative values if we have no moral standard to gauge by, and concepts blur for us. When God calls our name, He is calling us to be saved from a shifting-sand foundation to one of solid rock. Therefore, one of the things which happen for us when we hear God call our name is that standards stop fluctuating, and what is right and wrong becomes clear.

It is essential to understand that the Bible is considered a word from heaven given to humanity, yet one revealed through a Jewish cultural lens. Therefore, it only makes sense that the understanding of Hebrew is helpful to grasp all that the word from heaven is telling us. For example, in Jewish culture, a father was the only one who could name a child. Only he would decide what name this new child would bear for the rest of his or her life. Likewise, our Heavenly Father does the same because He is the one who names us. When we receive our God-given title, one of the things which happens right away is the restoration of our identity. When God calls us, we immediately know who we are.

Today, it is easy for us not to know our true selves. We are a people who suffer from confused identities, what our gender is, what our place in society is, or what we are born to do. We fall for every confusing ideology the world has to offer about our character, and like lost sheep, we wander into lands of trouble where we have no clue about our reality or to whom we belong. We remain in this state, lost in a foreign land until we are called by the One who names us. When the Heavenly Father whispers our name, it becomes clear, quite possibly for the first time, for whom we were made.

But how are we supposed to know what to do unless we grasp who we are, and how can we realize who we are unless we hear our name spoken by our Father? His heavenly cry removes the fog over us, revealing our true nature. We are to be sons and daughters of the Most High created to become beautiful people, and not to remain as unidentified slaves in a foreign country. There is now a specific place to where we belong and a specific family to whom we call our own.

God connects our identity through His *Beautiful Call*

Another thing which happens is that we become something new, and when I say new, I mean a creation that has not existed before.

We all know the phrase "like a baby's skin" to signify the smoothness of a newborn. A baby has not yet endured harsh weather, sunburns, cuts, bruises, scars, or other imperfections because it is born with perfect flesh. We marvel at its softness because, as we glance at our own, recognizing how old we ourselves have become. All our imperfections stand out, from wrinkles, age spots, brokenness, and the burden of time upon our muscles and bones.

There is the scar of our finger reminding us we were once too careless with a knife or a seared section of our arm when we touched something too hot. An enemy arises in a mirror, revealing our flaws, which we realize others also can see. It is the curse of aging. Yet, not so for the baby, which has that vibrant, smooth skin untouched by these downfalls of life on the earth we have endured.

The Beautiful Call: When God Reveals Our Name

What joy we would have if we could be new like one just born. It seems unlikely that we, who were once so scarred and broken, can experience a refreshing of newness.

Yet we can, for Jesus said we must be born again. When this happens, we are made fresh. The benefit of being born again states that old things have now passed away because the new has come. But what are these if they are not the scars of mistakes we have made in the past, where wrong choices have chiseled our features from patterns of sinful behavior. Old things are all the wounds we receive throughout life, and all those we inflict on others. Since others have wronged us, and we also them, guilt and unforgiveness poison our bodies. "Blame" for the troubles we have caused by our mistakes and "unforgiveness" for what was brought upon us by others have carried on stress and disease upon us where we could not let them go. It is the very thing that scars our flesh.

In our desperation, we cry out, "Are we to be forever in this condition of receiving and giving out such pain? Can anyone help us?" Hearing the Father's beautiful call changes all of the hurts and scars we have accumulated through our lives when we are born again. It clears the slate for us.

When we hear that heavenly voice whisper our name, a momentous shift occurs for us in the transition from old to new. It is a life restart which has an incredible side effect: it removes judgment of our past. Who does not want that?

Given this, all legal condemnation has a cease-and-desist order placed on our behalf when we receive Jesus as Lord and Savior. Because of being born again, our history is not allowed to work against us anymore. We cannot be convicted of our former things, given that Jesus fuses our past to the charges which lay against our old nature. That old nature is done away with forever. When the old was taken away, its charges were disposed of as well. It corrects our past through this procedure under the cross of Christ.

Even if we stumble in our new life, the cross gives us access to wipe them away, as if we had never sinned. All it requires for this to happen is repentance and the blood of Christ, which will wash us clean.

When Jesus died, we declared that it was good news. How is this so? How can we call death good? Because Jesus took the punishment due to our old, sinful lifestyles and paid the price for it. He purchased our life prison sentence from this world's judge and took our place where He did the time. In fact, He did all of our time.

Once prisoners have served their sentence, they say they have paid their debt to society bearing in mind that they have served or done their time. Since Jesus died for all, He did so much time that there was enough left over to change the timeline. If we look for ourselves, we will find this is so.

On the year Jesus was born, the calendar began to run forward, but up to that point, it ran backwards. Before Jesus came, we counted time back or counted down. When He came to purchase our sentence, which is why we hear the words "redeemed" or "purchased" because He paid the judge with His own life to step into our place, He changed our time to add good years to it.

We no longer count down on the calendar, as was done before Jesus came to the earth, but now we count upward. Until His time, we used to subtract the years, but now we add them. Where we once counted down to judgment, now we add years because we are counting up to something: His soon coming.

Being born-again is an over-the-top deal, entirely in our favor, paid for at the cost of heaven's resource. Technically, we call this grace. It is through grace alone that we are saved; this is why grace is amazing, and why we call it good that Jesus died for us.

Even more wonderful news is that genuine acceptance begins here. Jesus presents the adoption paperwork in heaven's court, lawfully making us part of God's family; He files them personally on our behalf, testifying to the fact that we are now His family. This action fulfills the Law, placing us legally into God's lineage through the grace of God. Being in God's family brings benefits we rarely consider. We now become benefactors of two covenants, both the old and the new.

Another unique thing that happens to those of us made new is that we become citizens of two worlds at the same time—both heaven and earth. We gain access to everything because we now sit in spiritual places, just like those who are already there. Rights and privileges are granted to us just as those in heaven have.

> *But God, who is rich in mercy, because of His great love with which He loved us, even when we were dead in trespasses, made us alive together with Christ (by grace you have been saved), and raised us up together, and made us sit together in the heavenly places in Christ Jesus.*
>
> – Ephesians 2:4–6, emphasis added

We become coheirs with Jesus Christ. Since He died on the cross, this means He has read His last will and testament, witnessed by everyone in heaven. It connects us with the benefits of Abraham's prior covenant, sealing the deal, and it is now in the books.

What He does next, however, is mind-blowing because He combines the power of the old promises with spiritual blessings of the new, creating one all-encompassing benefit package for us. We gain covenant blessing, healing, and provision through this brilliant arrangement, along with every limitless connection Jesus made about the kingdom of heaven.

> *Do not fear, little flock, for it is your Father's good pleasure to give you the kingdom.*
>
> -Luke 12:32

There is even more to this winning scenario than we can imagine because we venture into a governing system not of this world: the kingdom of heaven. We gain direct value as we become cemented into the richest, most powerful, most influential governing family of all time.

> *Our Lord Jesus Christ, who has blessed us with **every spiritual blessing** in the heavenly places in Christ,*
>
> – Ephesians 1:3, emphasis added

Grace empowers us, faith moves us, and our minds are renewed. We also get a regenerated spirit inside of us that communicates with the Holy Spirit, so in this, we are truly born again: once of water (natural birth) then born of the spirit (spiritual birth). Because the spirit is reborn inside of us, we begin to understand those things we could not even hope to fathom before. This concept is where life with God becomes exciting for millions who have had the experience of being "saved."

C. S. Lewis said, "The Son of God became a man to enable men to become sons of God."[3]

Hearing God call our name and responding to it allows us the outlandish privilege of becoming the sons and daughters of God. Paul, the apostle, said it this way:

> *And with everlasting life, how shall He not also give us all things?*
>
> *– Romans 8:32*

Once we become sons and daughters of God, we receive a purpose for why we are here on the earth. Now that God changed us by depositing eternal qualities within, He will send what He places inside of us to change the world outside of us. Once God has called our name, He will send us out by giving us a new name.

It is never a mistake; God never pocket dials us and says, "Oops, I called the wrong number." Look at who is contacting us. We know the Creator of heaven and earth has communicated with us, and we should ask, "Did You call me, Lord?"

Do not hold the call, answer it; this call is the most crucial opportunity we will have in our lifetime. If we let Him, God will "blow up our phone," as the saying goes, because He is very talkative. If we only learn to listen for the beautiful call of the Lord whispering our name, we will understand names mean something in the earth.

So, the question is: Have we heard the Beautiful Call?

5
The Beautiful Call

The audible whisper of God saying our name.[4]

No earthly words can describe it.

God uses a heavenly language when He speaks, and though it is beyond explanation, we can still hear Him. Somehow, from out of the silence, an undeniable message enters our hearts and minds, impressing us with His presence so actively we will not forget. When we first hear Him speak to us, it blows our mind until the Lord helps.

There is nothing like it when we figure out that God is addressing us directly because it makes us pause. We become very still as His voice places our cozy existence on a razor's edge. Our usual pace of life thrusts into an exhilarating realm full of heavenly rhythm ripe with unlimited possibilities as we come face to face with a living God.

Time itself acts differently, stepping aside as an unimportant thing. At the same time, the reality of speaking with someone beyond our realm blasts our expectations like a bomb, exceeding our normal limits since the physical cannot hold up against this kind of interaction.

Supernatural encounters create surreal moments.

In some ways, when God speaks to us, it is like we picture something going up, having expectations of it coming down, but it never does. Here, our mind fails to process what is happening. Why is that thing refusing to fall, defying the natural law of gravity, and why is it remaining suspended in air?

It is as if the action is saying, "Hey, look here. Let me get your attention." Our minds instruct us that what goes up must come down, yet, when the Lord calls, natural law must give way if He commands it do so. Therefore, when we hear His voice, it is as if we are staring at things hanging in mid-air, and we know we are witnessing something stupendous.

Talking to God is wondrous.

Natural laws move out of the way when the supernatural interacts with it. As the Lord talks to us, it is as if the laws of the physical world subdue, which is strange to our senses because we rely so heavily upon them. They have become second nature in everything we do, a foundation upon which we act, and yet, when they disappear, we no longer find something substantial to stand upon. It is why we do not understand how to act when we first encounter God, for He presents something to us with which we are unfamiliar. When He communicates, we see a different possibility as if He has opened up heaven for our review.

The Beautiful Call: When God Reveals Our Name

With the natural out of the way, eternity presents itself with bristling clarity. Everything is new and exotic as we see unlimited options, though we are untrained to process the experience. Whenever God speaks, time and nature bow low, and it interrupts our "normal" with the holy and spectacular. Natural laws do not hinder God when His presence passes by, as they kneel to His majesty like servants to His whims, and it is here where Jesus utters mysteries that we never knew existed.

As the spiritual meets the physical, it is overcome, and then God speaks. When the Red Sea was parted, God spoke; when the great fish swallowed Jonah, God spoke, and when Jesus walked upon the waters, God spoke.

The deed is done, the word is released, and it ransacks our average life as we lose the handle on our situation. It is as if the wind had rushed by, blown our hair about, and taken away what we once held firmly in our hands. We no longer can be satisfied with a lesser way of life. It leaves us with the impression that we have grappled with greatness.

God calls as heaven invites the earth. The Deity cries out to humanity just as holiness summons the unholy.

Simply put, God, who is over all, calls to us who are under all. It is wild, crazy, bold, and beautiful, but there is God openly speaking words to us, which we can hear.

Something about the call of the Lord reaches into our innerness and grabs us tight. It will not let us go, and we cannot fidget our way out of it. When He communicates from heaven, it fits into our soul like a hand slides into a glove. It is as if we had been designed for this encounter from the start.

During this interaction, we understand our purpose. We are made to talk to this One who is Strength, Wisdom, and Love all wrapped into one, and to respond to His voice. We recognize the ramifications when the Lord calls our name.

What can mere words say except the call of the Lord is beautiful? If we hear His voice, but once, we immediately know its truth, and that it lays beyond the capacity of human language to do justice to its beauty.

Some of us liken God's voice to a bell whose sole purpose is to proclaim liberty. Others think of it as honey, which is sweet to the taste. Yet, for many more, the voice of

The Beautiful Call: When God Reveals Our Name

God gives an understanding of mysteries, like a sea with no boundaries.

I say the voice of the Lord is beautiful, and it cannot be contained in the words of mortal man.

A whisper passes by, a call rings out, or a word plants secretly in our hearts; these are the movements of God's voice lightly heard and rarely experienced. However, once perceived, the hearing of it cannot be undone. It is like a woman who has been told her entire life that costume jewelry is sufficient—and she accepts this as fact until she lays her heart upon a genuine diamond. From that moment, no substitute would ever satisfy her again, and this is how it is when we hear God speak to us. Our value system reorders when we hear His voice, making things once so highly treasured, pale in comparison to the sound of Jesus calling our name. Nothing in this world is equal to the voice of God stirring in our ears.

Nothing.

As we live out our days, most of us have trials we despise and troubles we barely tolerate that threatens never to leave us with a moment's peace. We become worn, and our hope erodes like a canvas laid in the sun for too many years, forgotten and decaying to its ruin. "What purpose is there in living if this is all it has to offer?" we ask. Burdened under such broken mindsets, how can we bear to look up and see greater things if no superior decree is spoken before us? It is like settling for costume jewelry when real diamonds wait for the taking.

How can we hope to have something more if we do not even know a better thing is available? It is not on our grid, meaning we cannot realize the concept. So, this is the reason we need to hear the beautiful call of God's voice for in a flash we could visualize that thing which we could not otherwise have seen. By hearing Him, we can view beyond our limitations.

There was no creation until the Lord spoke because it takes His word to declare a future hope and a life worth living. God speaks of the more extraordinary thing so that we can expect good news, and He will announce the better thing to come, though it does not yet exist. His voice shatters the smoke-and-mirrors of this world's slavery-system, opening up limitless possibilities through His freedom. Only by His word can we break out of the sinister mindset determined to keep us laboring in the grind. This is not what we were made for; we were meant to be part of the royal family instead.

There is trouble in this life, which is a sure thing, but the comfort is that the voice of God will help us walk through it. This voice will give us lifesaving directions in dire circumstances, and provide revelation and support when we need those, too. Our life depends on hearing God's voice.

We are undone without a word from the Father's heart, and yet, when we finally hear it, we have been undone once more, because nothing shy of God's voice will ever do again.

When our hearts hear the call of a loving Father from heaven, we will never settle for the slavery of earth as our final destination, nor anything less than the "breaking out" of heaven upon the world in which we live.

It is a wild call, with power to smash cedar trees and melt the hardest hearts, yet it is musical, soft, and strong all at once. In a moment, God's voice can download into our spirits an eternity of understanding and purpose the way only a spiritual voice can do.

But most of all, it is beautiful, and in an instant, it can change death to life and fill our spirits like a wind fills a sail.

I am convinced God plants eternity into our hearts when we are children. After sewing it in us while we are young, when we water that seed, it will bear fruit, producing an eternal longing. This desire blossoms into our destiny.

To hear the voice of God is to come face to face with the beauty of another world from which we cannot hide for the rest of our lives. We have heard heaven's true call, and from there, nothing else will ever do.

And to think God is speaking to us every day; so, even more, we should listen for the beautiful call.

But be careful, do not be too busy to miss it.

Behind the Tree Where God Speaks

And the man who stood among the myrtle trees answered and said...

Zechariah 1:10

GOD SURPRISES US.

We do not know when He chooses to intersect with our lives. For some, this comes easily; but for others, we are blindsided when least expected. The latter was the encounter I had with God's voice.

I took note in Scripture how often God speaks around trees. Abraham met the Lord to bargain for cities at the trees of Mamre, Nathaniel sat under a tree where Jesus beheld him. Zacchaeus lodged in a branch as He passed by, so he was able to see the Messiah come to town. These were examples when Jesus intersected with people and trees. Still more exist as He cursed a fig tree and, of course, there is the Tree of Life. Something unique happens when God speaks near a tree, and now it was my turn to experience this personally.

The Lord planned to connect with me like a runaway train; I was about to be spiritually run over.

A businessman of nearly forty years, I regularly traveled to faraway places. Once, when consulting for business in the Florida Panhandle, I headed back to my hotel after a long day when colleagues planned to meet me for dinner. It was here, on the way, that God scheduled one of those blindsiding events on a seaside road just for me.

During this trip, I traveled scenic Highway 98, passing a mile-long stretch of roadway where blooming crape myrtles sat in the median. These trees produce large, showy flowers in whites, reds, and purples waving at the ends of their branches, a favorite for passersby.

Close to the coast, I drove past them spotting their blooms bobbing up and down in the typical sea breeze. Everyone in the area had seen them a hundred times and would as much again because these trees were found everywhere in the South, but I was more hungry than I was concerned about sightseeing, so my mind stayed on the upcoming dinner.

Nevertheless, God planned an intersection with me because He was about to pass by.

A whiff of something heavenly drifted by me, and I recognized the Holy Spirit's arrival when He changed the atmosphere in my car. He was trying to get my attention, and, of course, He succeeded.

Something thick with the presence of God pushed its way in, immersing me in the scene. An impression compelled me to look once more at those swaying blooms, and when I did, my gaze froze upon them.

What had been a natural breeze suddenly became an "unusual" one, and I could not glance away from those windy, dancing flowers.

While focusing on those huge blossoms moving in the wind, Eternity seemed to step in as information poured down into me like rain. This event came so quickly that nothing processed right away; it merely dropped in from above. Anyone who glimpsed my way would have noticed nothing strange because I drove on completing my evening, dinner, and all.

Though everything appeared normal on the outside, something unannounced had struck me, and I had no defense against whatever this was. In that spiritual altercation by the myrtle trees, I encountered a personal God so powerfully that its memory has never faded, even to this day.

Jolted profoundly, I was unsure by how much until God began to unpack these downloads later in the hotel room. Everything unfolded at a rate that I was able to manage, and this was how the interpretation started for me.

A vision began as though I were watching a movie. Over and over, I would see it, which would start again from beginning to end until I could recall it from memory. Each time I could remember a little more until I had it all.

The process was breath-taking, and I was held fast in place, feeling a little like a mad scientist had trapped me in a secret laboratory while pumping information into my overworked brain. I would say this was supernatural empowerment because of the energy-filled atmosphere, but all I could manage to do was sit still while the incident played again and again.

Compressed was the best word to describe what was happening. The Lord would continually display those dancing blooms, and each time He decompressed a layer of meaning. Through this method, all that God gave in a mere instant along Highway 98 opened to me.

Watching those branches swaying in an "unusual" breeze, I, like Moses, thought, "Let me turn aside and see this strange sight." From there, I heard a howling wind increase until its sound became the only focus.

It dominated the vision and at first appeared natural, but I soon understood that the roaring of this wind represented the noise of the world. This revelation was when God unlocked its spiritual meaning.

As the vision restarted, gusty sounds blared everywhere. While blossoms thrashed about like flags in a hurricane, the noise of the wind unexpectedly reduced. Again, this happened until the sound almost hushed even though the action was still happening. It was like someone began to turn down the soundtrack of a motion picture, while everything else was still moving. The sound eventually drained completely away.

At this junction is when I first heard it.

A new noise appeared on the scene, but it was an under-the-wind sound, so low in volume that I had to strain to listen. I even wondered if it existed at all, but I knew it was there.

The vision had two unique traits. First, the noise of the wind dropped every time it repeated, and second, a different sound rose in its place. This pattern continued until I overheard something spoken... barely. The sound came again, and I determined where the voice originated. Once more, the call grew in my ears, but this time I jumped by what I heard.

"Did someone just call my name?" I asked myself in surprise.

It was strange to the extreme because this rising call came from under the noise of the world.

Trying to listen beneath the clatter proved to be a strenuous exercise, but with focus, I succeeded enough to understand that my name was being spoken under the noise of the world. It was spoken so softly that I easily might not have perceived anything at all. Later, when I thought about this again, the Spirit explained, "Many times, the Lord calls us, and we let the noise of the world drown out His call because His voice is understated." It immediately affected me because I realized how often we let loud things block out His still small voice, costing us an opportunity to participate when God speaks.

Next, branches moved with vigor, as the noise continued to fade away. Aha! There it was! Unmistakably, I distinguished the call of my name as clear as a bell, sounding out pure and free. Without competition from the noisy wind, I was amazed at how loud the call had become as my name moved to the central part of what I was witnessing.

We recognize when someone's eyes fall upon us, and we know we are being watched. We can feel it burn into us. That was the feeling which shot through my entire being when I realized God was looking at me from heaven. I always understood God had knowledge that I existed, but at that moment, something was different. I was sure I was the only one He had fixed His eyes upon, and this made the hair stand up on the back of my neck.

The Beautiful Call: When God Reveals Our Name

Abruptly, the tree became even more animated than before, as if it were trying to distract me from this rising voice, but it did not work because the only thing which kept my attention was the calling of my name. I would catch it being spoken louder and louder each time, and an impression came to me that "something" was changing, and "something" was coming. The sensation I got was that an intensely personal confrontation was about to happen at any moment; it was imminent.

Until now, I had only observed the vision like I was sitting in a motion picture theater watching a blockbuster movie. It meant I was always outside looking in. However, it changed into a first-person point of view. Before, as the action happened, I had only witnessed it, but now I experienced everything.

Up to this point, the calling of my name held my attention until I spotted the swaying branches suddenly coming closer. The scene shifted around me as the space between the myrtle and myself shrunk. The tree was not moving towards me but rather vice versa, and a sense loomed that the "something coming" I recognized earlier had finally arrived. My spirit was excited within me as I scanned for whatever this "something" was, and that was the moment that I first laid eyes on Him.

Jesus stood on the other side of the tree as those blooms continued to bounce up and down, which equally revealed and hid parts of Him in their wind dance. It remained this way throughout the rest of the vision, and never was I given an unobstructed view of the Lord, nor did He look in my direction. Though not speaking to me, He did the oddest thing: He turned and walked away.

I struggled to see Him at times. Hoping to get a glimpse of Him without branches in the way, I saw that He walked behind the trunk of the tree. If I wanted to keep Him in sight, standing still would not do, and in trying to gain a clear spot, I knew had to follow.

Advancing on His position, I chased Him round, able to spot His waist and arm in motion. He was constantly moving and I could sense He was amused as He strode away. With determination I pushed ahead like a steam engine, I had to catch Him.

Just as I made some headway, one of those dancing myrtle flowers popped up in my face, much to my chagrin. With an angry grunt I shoved it out of the way, but the distraction was enough to let Jesus escape. My goodness was He ever elusive and I had to jog to get Him square in view again.

Walking around to the far side of the tree I could only make out a shoulder and hand; that is all that was visible, but I felt I was getting close. And if He did not dart around the trunk once more. I told myself if I wanted to see Him, I had to pace my advancement with His retreat.

Gushing winds shoved branches in front of me, diverting my path. This delay forced me to watch as Jesus stepped aside yet again. I wondered if He were toying with my pursuit because only an elbow here or a foot there could be seen at any time, just enough to keep me in the chase.

Like a merry-go-round, we circled the tree, bobbing up and down between branches, sure now that He wanted me to pursue. When meeting Jesus became more important than anything else, I could feel the confidence growing in me that

I could catch Him, so I sped on with sheer willpower. I was going to see Him with an unobstructed view.

When I caught back up with Him, all that lay between us was a final branch, so I closed in like a predator. Ducking out of sight for the last time, Jesus disappeared in my view. Yet I was convinced I had Him because I had gained position on Him over the past couple of turns. Clearing the last offshoot, I fully expected to see Jesus in the wide open.

I was about to step into a space unhindered by swaying blooms, where nothing would block my view again, and that was where I found myself. I could no longer see branches, dancing blossoms, or wind throwing things up in the air. Everything calmed down and became perfectly still as if this is the way it had always been. Behind the tree, I stood unopposed for the first time.

I could see Jesus nowhere, but I was not disappointed, for I was standing where I was supposed to be. From the chase, He brought me to the place where He wanted me to come.

Instead of being in the wide-open with the Lord, I stood in a beautiful garden, full of green grass and bright flowers overlaid with a caressing breeze, the kind I would have desired for a hammock's perfect midday nap.

This place was filled with everything which attracted me to it. Though no one told me directly, I knew this was my garden. If I wished for something, it was already available, prepared in advance because the One who made this paradise was intimately acquainted with my desires.

Everything overflowed with a peace so real that it wrapped around me like a warm blanket, soaking deep into my soul. It was the best I ever felt, and just trying think about it today immediately floods me with joy. Even though Jesus was not there, I was satisfied because I was in my garden, that sacred, secret place where nothing was wrong nor out of sorts. It was created for me alone, and I knew that deep within. For out of all the billions of people who had ever lived, no one had this exact spot because this was, of course, mine, and it was prepared by the One I desired to see the most.

To the left, a path ran out to where a stone bench sat in the open light, where it was illuminated by wondrous rays. A peaceful warmth flowed out like a river, affecting me though I was still far away, and here was the kind of location that the

Lord was sure I would love. "This," I thought to myself, "was the kind of place I would want to go where I could ponder mysteries, think great thoughts, and worship Jesus."

As comfort swept over my emotions, and I normalized so I could take it all in, I could not think how it could be more perfect. Nowhere else might I imagine laying down in complete safety due to the thick peace here. No troubling thought could approach me because living contentment continually washed all my worry and fear away as a waterfall does to sand in a river; it merely carried them far from me.

Where I stood, trouble offered no fight, reminding me of how that flowing water sweeps pebbles away with little effort. It was no trouble to move my trouble away.

The Lord created this little Eden for me with His own hands, and I recall never wanting to leave. Since this was where I was meant to be, feeling no shame, remorse, or sin, but only total acceptance, the feeling immersed me that I had come to my real home.

A spiritual something was in place that mere words were unable to describe, and to me, it had the "it" factor. It had the "me" factor because this was my Eden.

The Beautiful Call: When God Reveals Our Name

Surveying the landscape on the backside of the myrtle, I understood it was more than a vision because I found a secret place behind a tree where God would speak. It was a secret oasis the world could never enter, but I could.

I found out almost 15 years afterward that Scripture does not mention the myrtle tree until the time God's people were carried away into captivity. The Lord used this tree as a symbol of recovery,5, and the vision presented itself fittingly to me personally, but I have the sense that this would apply to everyone as well. If we feel captive in some horrible scenario, look for a myrtle tree, and it will remind us that God has promised to remove us from our captivity and place us in His promised land.

He prepared still waters and green meadows for me, just like the one David saw in Psalm 23. I stood in a garden where Jesus and I would meet at future times, only the two of us, where I would learn great mysteries.

This secret place would reveal the mysteries of God and be full of beautiful moments, far away from the loud noises of a troubling world. It was also here where I met a Man who called me from the myrtle trees. I found a home behind the tree where God speaks.

And just like that, it was over.

The whole event centered around God calling my name

A verse in a Christian song by DeGarmo & Key,[6] entitled *Talk To Me*, focuses on how God has us standing next in line, and what great hope is that during a trial?

When all else turns against us, knowing that we are next in line to receive our answer from God, speaks hope that we are not forgotten. On the contrary, it confirms our coming promise and chases our desperations far away as the east is from the west.

Though we have waited for a long time, when the person in front of us has their name called, our excitement grows because we know we are next.

The Beautiful Call: When God Reveals Our Name

To this, we say, "It is about time." Our time has come, and it is about time to listen to God speak because He has something to say to us that is critical, essential and life changing.

The Lord would use a tree for me again when one day, I came home a different path from work. I was looking for a way out of my current rut and found myself on a street that I had never been on before. That is when I saw a beautiful home with even more lovely trees all around.

Amazed at the beauty of the area, I said in my heart, "These trees are magnificent." Drawn to the property, God said, "The glory is behind the tree," and I knew precisely what that meant. In thirty days, that house became my new home and a place where the Lord would speak glorious things to me. Because there were so many trees on the property, I did not notice the most important one of all.

One morning, almost a year later, I opened the curtain in the master bedroom, on my side of the room, and realized there was a myrtle tree in full bloom. It was framed like a wall hanging, perfectly placed. It had been there all along, yet I never noticed until now. Blossoming with the same color as I what I had seen in the vision years earlier, it suddenly dawned on me that importance of the "Jesus" Tree. He planted it at the house by the widow where each night I would lay my head. It was here that God would speak mysteries to me in my dreams, wake me up with a whisper of wisdom in the morning before I started my day, and He knew in advance that one day I would live here. It had been planted before it was my desire, had been planned from the start, and surely was a God moment. This house is full of them because I once heard the beautiful call.

The Lord can make a secret place anywhere He chooses. What became a tree where God whispered my name for me could become our closet, bedroom, or garden. Wherever it is for us, we can find a secret place with Him there.

If we will seek Jesus and pursue Him with passion, then equally, He promises to design a place filled with the things for which our desires thirst. The task is to overcome the world's "noise" and listen to His still, small voice evoking our name.

If we perceive it, then this verse comes real for us - though it is always true.

The Beautiful Call: When God Reveals Our Name

> *You will keep him in perfect peace, whose mind is stayed on You because he trusts in You.*
>
> - Isaiah 26:3

I pray that we all begin to distinguish the voice of the Lord if we have not already, and if we have heard Him, that we find our garden from where we will exchange the secrets of heaven and earth with the Lord.

It arrests us when God whispers our name under the noise of the world. Is that the wind we hear now?

And this is only the first call, for God makes another. Imagine what will happen when He makes the second call.

Brian Louis Perkins

The Second Call
– Destiny

> *[God] who has ... called us with a holy calling, **...according to His own purpose** ...before time began...*
>
> 2 Timothy 1:9, emphasis added

God has a destiny planned for us.

When we think of a calling on one's life, the general idea includes every believer. We are a people invited to come out of the darkness and march boldly into the light (1 Peter 2:9); the Lord calls us from death to life (John 3:16), and ultimately from earth to heaven. We are also invited to live a holy life (2 Thessalonians 4:7).

But another call exists, which is more specific. There is a commission meant for us on an individual level, of which first comes to mind: a call to preach, or a missionary to some far-off land. We walk down the road of life, and one day, out of the blue, God pops onto the scene with a random appointment to do something we were not expecting. That is how we think of a call, but it is not how the Lord does, for He defines it differently.

Consider that Jesus appointed Peter, after His crucifixion, to establish His church. Likewise, He elected Paul to bring the gospel to the Gentiles. In the Old Testament, the word of the Lord was entrusted to Jonah to preach to the Ninevites, while giving unique power to Jeremiah and Isaiah in the office of prophets.

In the same vein, the Lord anointed David to be a king when he was only a shepherd and established Esther to be a queen to save a nation from annihilation. These are only a few examples among many which show specific calls throughout Scripture.

Having now understood this call, a question begs to be asked: What is destiny?

This word is knocked around like a ping-pong ball these days because it has become popular in modern culture.

Everyone and everything talk about life's purpose, but why do we do it?

The reason is that we get a sense that things are wrapping up in this world of ours, and we perceive the earth is in deep turmoil.

There is trouble over here and more worries over there, racial unrest creeps around every shadow while class warfare and pandemics move openly in the streets. A fight rages over such concepts as climate change, the green movement, and eco-friendly "sciences."

The earth is reeling, which pushes some of us to go into a Save-the-Planet mode. Understand this: the world is vital in the scope of the believer in Christ though we do not worship it like the Wiccan (witchcraft/witches) do. Nevertheless, we connect to it in another way in which they cannot for there is a link between the earth and the Christian.

Big secrets are profound to those who find them, so let us unpack one of these hidden truths ourselves: The earth is waiting for us.

The planet is "acting up" because it recognizes the time has come to be liberated from its bondage, and it is struggling to be free. If you have ever seen a dog rolling on the carpet, scratching its ears, rubbing its back on the ground to get rid of fleas, then you get the idea of what the earth is doing. Sin is the flea the planet is trying to get rid of, and it convulses and moves to be liberated. Even so, during this time, the sinful say the righteous are the world's problem, but it is quite the other way around.

> *For the creation was subjected to futility, not willingly, but because of Him who subjected it in hope, because the* **creation itself also will be delivered from the bondage of corruption** *into the glorious liberty of the children of God. For we know that the whole* **creation groans and labors with birth pangs** *together until now.*
>
> Romans 8:20-22, emphasis added.

The world groans for our revealing as the children of God because it knows that when we are free, it will be also. We also feel there is some connection between the "end of the world" drama we experience today, and the purpose to which we are being called to as believers. We have a future of greatness coming, and this world knows it.

Still, the question remains: What is destiny?

The world defines this term as "what is meant to be"6, linking it to a future foretold as in a fortune teller7, or an inescapable series of future events.

But God defines this quite differently. With Him, there is always an escape.

> *No temptation has overtaken you except such as is common to man;* **but God is faithful**, *who will not allow you to be tempted beyond what you are able, but with the temptation will also make* **the way of escape**, *that you may be able to bear it.*
>
> 1 Corinthians 10:13, emphasis added

According to ungodly sources, destiny is something fused within us that we cannot avoid such an inescapable fate7, but God's definition is again different; He always gives a free choice in the matter. Our purpose, while outlined by the Lord, is something not set in stone like karma. Rather it is a privilege which we can rise to, yet, it is one we can surely miss. We must decide to grab a hold of our calling but never is it unavoidable, as a lot of us go to our graves, neglecting what we were born to do. Many preachers have testified how they ran from their callings until they had a change of heart.

God has made us agents of free will, and because of this, we have a choice. We can choose to run, deciding to never align with our destiny, but that is not an advisable course of action. It would be better if we allowed the Maker of heaven and earth to fill our sails and allow the wind to take us to the place that He desires us to be.

Providence sings the song of what we were created to do, and our hearts are instantly drawn to its melody because our souls recognize the tune. We have been trying to sing this life song, and here God comes along, bringing the sweet refrains we have been missing since our time began.

This thing we were created to do will be tailor-made, and in it, we will function joyfully and efficiently. A strong, willful act would be required to separate ourselves from what seems to fit us so perfectly.

Our story is written down in heaven, and we have a "calling" for its performance. It may simply be to live a holy life as an example before an unholy world. Maybe we are to shine as a light in a dark place or as complex as to champion a heavenly cause such as revival or salvation. It may be specific and situational for a particular time, like Queen Esther, to whom we quote the famous line, "Who knows that you weren't born for such a time as this?" (Esther 4:14).

These are God's stories to write over us as He did for Esther, and as He did for the prophet Jeremiah.

> *Before I formed you in the womb, I knew you; before you were born, I sanctified you; I ordained you a prophet to the nations."*
>
> Jeremiah 1:5

The Lord has a plan for our life, whether to preach, teach, evangelize, or be a light in an unlit place - whatever our calling may be. God wrote down in heaven what we were to accomplish on the earth even before we were born. Therefore, as we begin to function in our destiny, the common saying becomes real, "This is what I was born to do!"

God carefully wires us in a certain way as not to let us blend into other pursuits easily, though we try to force the issue with our willpower. However, when we learn our God-given destiny, we move in it with incredible strength and purpose. We are amazed at how well we adapt into the role, even against extreme resistance as if we have some secret experience only now activated. We are in the flow right away; actions seem intuitive, and difficulties become joyfully doable. It appears as if we have been managing the new thing all our lives from the way we are functioning with it. What is this strange power within us which lets us operate so adeptly with something in which we have no experience?

We become like a hull of a boat when it finds the water it was designed to cut through. It has lain in dry dock being made ready for its big moment but from the day it is launched it immediately finds its way at the onset. There is no training required for it to do what it was made to do. Effortlessly, the vessel runs the ocean as if it were a razor cutting paper. It is how it will be for us when we discover our purpose, efficiently and powerfully utilizing it as sure as the lines of a ship are to the sea beneath. We have a precise flow when we know we have been perfectly placed.

Our spirit validates where we should be and what we should do, and it sparks life within us as we accomplish the very thing for which heaven designed us. The Spirit of God confirms our assignment because we will be called forth, called upon, and called into action to do it.

Are we to sing? Are we to worship? Will a nation be set in our path? Will we write a book? Is there a sermon we are to preach? Or is there a divine appointment for us to meet one world-changing person?

God has a personal opportunity for us, and we will engage in it when He calls our name.

The Beautiful Call: When God Reveals Our Name

Listen, because it is the Father's heart toward us where we will be given our calling and hear what our future will be. Once we receive it, then we do what He has done, making callings all our own. He may use us to call others to arms, an "all hands-on deck" hail, or "calling all cars" moment needed to save the day.

We may direct others to their place in the kingdom. But we may also be the one which declares truth into a world of lies or someone who calls things as we see them.

We may be the one God uses to make the tough call, where desperate times call for drastic measures.

And as we will shortly see, through us, God may call the devil's bluff, make him lay his cards on the table and then call him to the carpet.

Ultimately, destiny is a beautiful plea where God is signaling outstanding men and women to come to their service, but only a few will listen.

Many are called, but few are chosen.

Matthew 20:16

Have our heartstrings been pulled by God Himself? We should respond because this is the most important call we will ever answer.

The Beautiful Call: When God Reveals Our Name

Brian Louis Perkins

6
The Name-Caller

> *The reputation (name) of the righteous leads to blessing...*
>
> -Proverbs 10:7 ISV, note added

GOD IS A NAME-CALLER.

When He calls our name, we are stricken in our path and unable to ignore it because when God speaks to us, we are impressed that life is about to change in an unforeseen way.

Abram was a man who lived in an idol infested land and connected at the hip to his father. God directed him to leave his city and family for a new country, but he did not sever all ties until his father died. Finally, he left and would go on to make mistakes along his journey, but God was faithful and helped him in a way he could not foresee.

> *No longer shall your name be called Abram, but your name shall be Abraham; for I have made you a father of many nations.*
>
> - Genesis 17:5

God does this to us all: He gives us new names. Abram became Abraham, which is a name the world still remembers after almost 4000 years. Later, his grandson Jacob would also have a unique name as well.

> *And He said, "Your name shall no longer be called Jacob, but Israel; for you have struggled with God and with men and have prevailed."*
>
> - Genesis 32:28

We find examples of God changing a believer's name throughout the Bible. Eventually, Saul, a terrorist toward believers, became Paul, the beloved apostle who taught the church into his last years, writing most of the New Testament. His name change moved him from killing Christians to dying himself for the cause that he once persecuted, sealing his destiny with a witness of his sacrifice. When God begins to "name-call" us, we change, because our prophetic name unveils something about the purpose to which God made us.

We transform into what our God-given name reveals about our calling.

When God appeals to us by this new name, we receive the beautiful call of significance and take on the destiny contained in His appeal. God's call rewrites our DNA into what He destined us to be. The spiritual realm knows our name; angels are aware of it, devils know, the great cloud of witnesses understand it, too, and so does God. These are automatic because names mean something in the heavenlies, but the genuine breakthrough comes when we learn it ourselves.

This name-calling from the Lord is a process that transforms us into who He means us to be.

The phrase, "name-calling," has harmful undertones because of its connection with negative impacts. As a child, we remember being called names with painful effects, where blows we took from those words bruised our souls. Even today, we are offended when people call us a name because we rage back to them, "Don't label me this or that." At the most inopportune time, name-calling can have a direct impact on our personality or mental state, threatening to shove us off the tracks with a single verbal jab.

Think about this. We become upset when we are called a bad name that holds a negative meaning. We do not use selected words for some cultures, jobs, or stations in life, and likewise, neither do we do this for body types - hair or skin color, weight, or height. We refrain from inflicting damaging word-punches to others because they are impactful.

Name-calling contains capability

In society, we face adverse consequences if we call someone a name, and one of the chief reasons is because name-calling affects identity. Whether we use or abuse them, names connect with personality, and they have the power to change a person.

In our younger days, we might have been called "stupid," "ugly," "fat," or other derogatory labels that shook us for a time and, honestly, still influences us today because of the strength names have upon us.

Ulysses Grant was called "Useless" Grant as a child, and later when he entered West Point Academy, an erroneous pen stroke gave him an unfamiliar "S" middle initial. His full name was Hiram Ulysses Grant, but he would become known as Ulysses "S." Grant, or simply U.S Grant.

He stewarded a war campaign for Lincoln and the Union army freeing all Americans regardless of their skin color, and he was useless no more for he would follow up that victory with one of another kind: as President.

Words are so important, yet we teach our children that "sticks and stones may break our bones, but words can never hurt us." The truth is that negative name-calling injures our fragile egos. The world is suffering from mass identity bruising, and one of the results from this soreness is instant offense, or what we call "being thin-skinned."

Truth is we are a bruised people and identity sore.

> *A bruised reed He will not break, and smoking flax He will not quench...*
>
> Matthew 12:20

If we genuinely grasped the importance of words, we would understand Jesus, because out of all the things that Jesus choose to be identified with, the Word was that one thing. The Word stood with the Father in the beginning, and the Word is God Himself.

The Lord believes words vitally act on our behalf for He led James, the brother of Jesus, to write:

> *Let your "Yes" be "Yes," and your "No," "No," lest you fall into judgment.*
>
> James 5:12

Often teachers use this verse to tell us not to talk too much or make our sentences short, but that is not what James explains here. Look at the scripture carefully. James is telling us that when we say "Yes," let this mean a "Yes," and likewise, when we say "No," let that be a, "No." God was not saying to limit our speech, but to make our words be found valid. We would declare in our culture, "Say what we mean."

Words enforce power and importance.

Consider Helen Keller, who was both deaf and blind, acting like a terror until a teacher was able to impart her one life-changing word. She testifies when she was taught the term "water" and realized the connection to a real liquid substance, she knew a thing called language existed. It was instantaneous by a single word.

Helen Keller records in her autobiography, "That living word awakened my soul, gave it light, hope, joy, set it free..."[9] She wrote this because she proved from her testimony words are impactful.

If we find this difficult to believe, why are we always seeking what someone else says about us, or more spiritual, why are we chasing a word from the Lord? Because, like Helen Keller, that one word can change our lives forever.

Names are specific words, and therefore, are more consequential.

Our heavenly Father has a name to speak over us, which drastically affects our persona. He has a name connected to who we are, whether we are a prince or princess, a healer, prophet, or deliverer. He intends to overwrite fleshly names heaped upon us from unloving sources, transitioning us to ones more fitting for our role in His kingdom. It ties us to what God calls us to do on earth.

The Lord is name-calling us into His image and our destiny.

We will become what the Lord declares that we will become.

Now look at two of the promises for the overcoming church in the book of Revelation; they are about names:

The Beautiful Call: When God Reveals Our Name

> *He who overcomes... I will confess his name before My Father and before His angels.*
>
> *- Revelation 3:5*

> *"He who has an ear, let him hear what the Spirit says to the churches. To him who overcomes I will give... a white stone, and on the stone a new name written which no one knows except him who receives it."*
>
> *- Revelation 2:17*

When God calls us by our prophetic name, it elevates us, taking us to our rightful place beside Him in the heavenlies.

Our prophetic name is important in the spiritual because it speaks of identity. When we are born again, we get new authority in the heavenlies, and all perceive it, usually before we do. The angels in heaven are rejoicing over our new name; the demons of hell are aware also. In the account of the seven sons of Sceva, the devil said, "Jesus, I know, and Paul, I know, but who are you?" (Acts 19:15). Because the enemy did not recognize the identity of these men, the devil beat them, stripped them naked, and they ran fleeing for their lives.

The spiritual realm is aware if we have an identity or not. Our prophetic names move us from servanthood to sonship, and where we are called to occupy a position in the kingdom as a child of God, we receive with it the authority to which God assigns. All heaven reacts to the name of Jesus, and all heaven will respond to the name Jesus gives us.

Names are famous in the spiritual realm, and God is a Name-Caller. What name has the Name-Caller spoken over us?

The Beautiful Call: When God Reveals Our Name

7
Our Second Name

> *You shall be called by a new name, which the mouth of the Lord will name.*
>
> -Isaiah 62:2

G<small>OD GIVES US A SECOND NAME.</small>

He attaches a destiny to it. But what is this "second name," and why have we not heard about this before? We might have come across this concept more often than we think but have not connected the dots when it has been taught.

Peter "the Rock" is the name he received after his original because his first was Simon. Saul became Paul, while Belteshazzar's name turned into Daniel. Each of these had one given to them, different from their birth name.

Sometimes the names we are born with are kept, but we add a title as it was for John. Jesus dubbed him "a son of thunder," but he grew into John, "the Beloved," or John, "the Revelator." They only knew Eve as "the woman" and Adam as "the man," but each got a new name; for example, Eve means "mother of all the living."

Sometimes the new name eclipses the original because of the power God lays upon it. Moses kept his name but moved from being a "prince of Egypt" to a "deliverer of Israel," and later, the "law-giver." Samuel, who was a temple intern, became a priest over a nation, and the one who would have the distinct honor to announce the start of the lineage of the coming Messiah. There was also David, a shepherd boy, who transformed into the "Giant-killer" and eventually became Israel's greatest king.

Our first name carries our identity, but the second holds our destiny.

The Beautiful Call: When God Reveals Our Name

God wrote this new name in heaven before He formed us in our mother's womb, and He dreamt of us before we were born. Destiny is the intention for which God made us.

We have an inner desire to discover our function in life, driving questions like, "Why am I here? What's my purpose?" Deep down, we want to understand this answer, and if delayed in reaching our goal - that thing we are supposed to do – then we feel sorely out of place. If we do not align with our created purpose, we wander out of joint with the world, moving from this group to that, never seeming to rest anywhere. It culminates to the point of misery because something inside of us yearns that our destiny is activated. God wired us to grow into what He made us for, and our souls know when we are not in alignment with our God-given direction. Until we enter into what we are meant for, we bear heaviness.

We only need to emerge as that thing we are supposed to be and walk in it, but the next question is, "How do we find our purpose? Who can show us the reason we are on this earth? How does this activate in us?"

As we search throughout the world, forcefully looking into relationships, wealth, power, and fame to become what we desperately seek, we discover our destiny only begins when the Lord's beautiful call registers within us.

He whispers out our name once to attract our attention in this world, but He calls it a second time to get us to look at another.

If we settle for this place alone, we have missed something grander. The Lord calls our name a second time so we can gaze upon another world.

8
Stuck Between Two Names

> *For where there are envy, strife, and divisions among you, are you not carnal and behaving like mere men?*
>
> I Corinthians 3:3

At first, everyone loves milk.

However, the older we become, many of us grow to be lactose intolerant. Milk is for babies and not so much for adults, though it is still a good thing. Our bodies will begin to reject too much of an infant diet while we are maturing. The problem is that many of us are stuck in the "milking phase." We have never been weaned off of it and are only accustomed to soft spiritual diets. Where we are content to consume comfortable foods, we eventually need something more substantial, physically, and spiritually.

No one who is fifty years old drinks from a baby bottle in the physical world, this would not be normal behavior. Nevertheless, in the spiritual, staying on infant diets way too long is quite common. A pastor early on in my Christian walk used to joke with his congregation that he has to change a lot of diapers on older people, insinuating many need to grow up in their faith.

When God calls us the first time, He speaks to our physical name or the name by which we are known in this world, and this is the call by which we are saved. However, He will call us a second time by the name we are known of in heaven, and this leads us into our destiny. The first call is for the earthly, the second is for the spiritual, and this is the intended progression of our faith.

But sometimes we are lost in a land between two names. We have heard our name the first time and received salvation for our souls, but we have never heard the next mention of our purpose. We are believers who languish in a middle ground, wallowing in "out-of-control" emotions producing few if any fruit of the Spirit.

Paul said to the Corinthians, I should be able to speak to you as mature Christians by now, but you are still acting like newborns.

The Holy Spirit longs to produce fruit in us, and Jesus looks for that fruit. Look at how he treated a tree that did not bear its fruit.

And seeing from afar a fig tree having leaves, He went to see if perhaps He would find something on it. When He came to it, He found nothing but leaves, for it was not the season for figs. In response, Jesus said to it, "Let no one eat fruit from you ever again. "And His disciples heard it.

*Now in the morning, as they passed by, they saw the fig tree **dried up from the roots**.*

Mark 11:13-14, 20 emphasis added

Jesus goes to look at our fruit we produce when we are mature enough to "have leaves." If we have been in the faith long enough to produce an image of a Christian, we should bear the fruit of one as well.

We know we are saved, but we have no idea what our purpose in life is, so we wander, straying into this trouble spot or another as children who are not yet taught. Without instruction, we do not root ourselves in a place long enough to produce fruit the Lord wants to see. We argue and strive with brothers and sisters, and leave this church or that, pulling up our roots. Without roots, there will be no fruit-production, at least not the kind God is looking for to emerge out of our faith.

Think about this again.

When God calls our name in the beginning, it is about us. We receive our identity as children of God, and this is who we are. In this phase, we function mostly about ourselves, our needs, and what God or our church can do for us.

However, the second time, it is for what we can do for Him, and not ourselves.

Our second name is where we receive our purpose, our calling, and it is not who we are but what we can do.

Those who seem to be carnal around us are those who seek to have God answer prayer only about themselves. It is still good in the sense that we have learned to come to God for our needs and brings us to one level of faith. But we need to grow from there and should not be stuck in the first name call. These are the people who have not heard the second call.

When we mature beyond the need to only pray about ourselves, then our prayer becomes about us and others, not us alone. Notice that mature believers still pray for their own needs. Praying in this manner does not change, nor is it done away with, but also, it adds something. Experienced believers, who have heard the second call from the Lord, also pray for others. It is a little different than praying for others in this respect; when adult believers pray for their own needs, they also believe to see a breakthrough for others when they get their provision. They want to be the breaker so that not only are their own needs met, but freedom, provision, and peace abound all around. Their answer is big enough to provide for many.

To minister to the needs of others than ourselves is the purpose of fruit; our fruit is not for us. We do not eat our fruit because it is intended for someone else. Our peace, joy, and long-suffering, mercy, etc., is for someone else to be blessed, and likewise, like any tree, we should have many fruits, not just one. There should be enough for all.

This kind of response happens when God calls our heavenly name, our spiritual name, our prophetic name, or our name of destiny. We enter our season to produce the excellent work of the Spirit. At this point, when we receive answered prayers, it affects our surroundings, and it sets many free. Our troubles are more prominent; our prayers are more significant, and so are our answers because they answer problems for more than just us. That is part of the grand design of God's beautiful call.

Yet, many of us live whole seasons without realizing our identity, let alone our purpose. I was this person and should have written this book decades ago, but I did not understand how stuck I was between an earthly and heavenly name. I received a saving faith, had a personal relationship with the Lord, even felt like I was on fire for God, but I did not mature as expected, drifting into a much later season than I should have. To bear expected fruit took longer for me because I failed to mature on schedule. This delay can cause us not to find our place at our time.

Trusting or not trusting the Lord moves or stops us, and some of us have stopped, becoming stuck between two names.

9
Names Mean Something
in the Spiritual

"...But who are you?"

Acts19:15

Names mean something in the spiritual realm.

My employer called me to a meeting where I knew they would fire me from the company. The writing was on the wall because the new owners came into clean house, bringing in their people to replace those of us who had been there for five years. They fired each of the former management team, one by one, and now it was my turn to face the chopping block. I ended up traveling an hour to get the unwelcomed news.

While at home, preparing for the dreaded trip, my wife and I were praying in our bedroom, agonizing over the looming event. Unexpectedly, I felt the Lord's presence enter the room as if He leaned over and spoke behind me. What He released to me was so strong that the hair on my head moved as if He were inches away when He spoke it. I felt the force in those words; His breath was that close. Startled, I jumped like a flaming iron touched my skin. When I shot up, it was not with a hallelujah, but with instant anger, I was hot and ready to fight over what I just heard.

What did God tell me which could provoke that kind of response? Why was I so upset? The reason was that I heard the Lord call me a name, and I did not like it one bit.

There was an insult tied to what He just said because He called me Jonah!

Of all the random things! Jonah was no more on my mind than if I thought I was the king of England. It was not on my radar, and angrily said to myself, "How dare He put that on me!"

We all know Jonah as the runaway prophet, but I was not running away from anything. "The nerve," I said to myself. "Here I am a Sunday School teacher, after all; I mean, I ran the soundboard, mowed the church lawn, and worked in the youth department," along with a list of other "notable actions" that I brought up in my defense to counter this offending charge. How could I be running from God?

I tried to justify myself in the Lord's presence. The perceived insult offended me like fiery coals, for I was inevitably hot. Like the prophet Jonah, I believed I understood more than God. See how quickly I took on the calling's nature? I was already acting like him (Jonah 4:1).

It took some time to cool down, and by "some time," I mean weeks and months. Eventually, though, I considered there might be another reason the Lord called me that forsaken name. If there was, I wanted to know, and this led me on a decade long journey to study all things concerning Jonah. Well, God had branded me, right? So, who was I to resist? I might as well go with it to find out what I could.

I studied the book bearing the prophet's name every chance I got and did this passionately year after year. During one stretch, I listened to three sermons a day about him.

I was learning much about what the Lord was trying to say concerning a man who led a revival. All I knew at that point was that I was undoubtedly being affected by the name the Lord called me. I was hearing the voice of God inspire me to find out why He burdened me with that name. I wrote everything down about the great fish-riding prophet that I had learned and was overwhelmed by the amount of wisdom that came out of a little four-chapter book.

After a thousand pages of notes, I still was not finished — all of this from a little book in the Bible, which only had forty-eight verses. Stunned at the outcome, I finally gave up and agreed that the biblical account of Jonah was inexhaustible, because I knew I could go on searching decades more and still find new things to consider.

Scripture is as deep as the sea into which they threw Jonah. I wore myself out plunging into the story, as surely as Captain Ahab thrust his spear into the whale named Moby Dick; It spent me.

Discovering deep understandings along the way, an odd thought crept into my mind about why God called me after a wayward prophet. It never occurred to me from the start how spectacular this runaway missionary to Nineveh was. It was a revelation how principled, and indeed misunderstood he was, and that the Lord loved him much. Jonah was the only man for the job, even though he did not initially want it.

From that moment on, Jonah held a special place in my heart, where once I thought to be insulted through association with his name, I now honor it.

God was not calling me out as a runaway, but something different than expected, and isn't that just what the Lord does? He did not insult me, as I first supposed, but gave me a prophetic call to the ministry of Jonah.

Names mean something in the spiritual

The Lord called Jonah to go to the most unpopular people, producing what is still known today as the most significant revival in world history.

Now that was something into which I could sink my teeth. My wife and I have moved our career track, housing location, and spiritual diet to position ourselves for the great harvest to come, all because names mean something in the spiritual realm.

Brian Louis Perkins

The Beautiful Call: When God Reveals Our Name

Brian Louis Perkins

Jonah and a Rock

[King Amaziah] restored the territory of Israel... according to the word of the Lord God... which He had spoken through His servant Jonah...

- 2 Kings 14:25

There is something about Jonah.

Most have not seen that he has spiritual attraction coming from his life. He had already achieved the status of being a seer by prophesying the restoration of lost national borders, so we ask, "Why is religious *attraction* news?" was not he already a spiritual powerhouse?

He was not only the mouthpiece of God, but he also enjoyed national fame since what he predicted had occurred. From the king on down, the Lord established him as the genuine article, so he was not only a prophet but a hero, as well.

We need to dig deeper than the surface to find rare jewels hidden beneath, and that is how it is for this revelation of Jonah.

A second directive came to him to travel to Nineveh, the city of gentiles, and this command connects with someone in the New Testament. In other words, he had a similarity to another person in the Bible.

Fast forward to a particular fisherman some eight hundred years later, and we find the link: Simon. Walking upon earthly shores, Jesus meets Peter face-to-face and calls him to "Come and follow," and the rest is history.

We know him as Peter today, but he had other names in the past. Simon served as his given name, but he also carried the tag of "the son of John," where John was a variant of Jonah. Some versions of Scripture read it this way, "Son of Jonah."

Interestingly, the name Simon in Hebrew means "he has heard." How appropriate was this name since it became prophetic? Simon caught the call of the Savior, and we can imagine that from all the fishermen in history, we only remember Simon because he listened to the Nazarene's words. Is that not something extraordinary since his name means "he has heard"?

> *Now when Jesus looked at him, He said, "You are Simon, **the son of Jonah**. You shall be called Cephas" (which is translated [Peter], A Stone).*
>
> - John 1:42 emphasis, notes added

Scripture says that when Jesus met Simon, He stood still and fixed His gaze upon him. Today, we might say the Lord gave him the once over. After Jesus did this, He did a very mysterious thing: He immediately gave Simon a new name.

He did not wait several months to find out Simon's character, or how he would respond to miracles, hard teachings, or trials, Jesus gave Simon a new prophetic name right away.

"You shall be called Cephas."

Cephas means "rock" or "stone." In Greek, Cephas is translated Petros or Peter and is the name by which the world knows him today. With all the millions of people throughout history, and alive today, who have been named Peter, it is a striking thing that when someone mentions this name, apostle Peter is the first one who comes to mind. What a lasting name the Lord gave him because names mean something in the spiritual.

Of course, Jesus told Peter that Peter would be the rock upon which the church would be built. Catholics take this as Peter himself being that rock, whereas Protestants say it was more his confession; regardless, whatever stance we take, Peter is associated with what Jesus called him. His prophetic name fulfilled his destiny. The church, which was born under his guidance, remains to this day, much like his name, a rock.

Jesus gave him another name after he had confessed that Jesus was the Son of the living God (Matthew 16:16). The Lord marveled and replied, "Blessed are you, Simon son of Jonah, for this was not revealed to you by flesh and blood, but by my Father in heaven" (v. 17).

Peter was called Simon, the "son of Jonah." Now, Simon Peter's father was John, also called Jonah (for John is a variant of Jonah), making this a factual statement by Jesus, but it was also a prophetic one.

Some disagree this is so, in past theological critiques[8], saying Jesus was only calling him a son of his earthly father. Still, after a decade of study, I have concluded Jesus was laying upon Peter the mantle of the prophet Jonah, and here is why I believe that.

Jonah went to the gentiles when it was unpopular; Peter did the same, for he went to the house of Cornelius the Gentile. Peter said to go to a Gentile's house was an unclean act, yet true to his character, he went after the Lord showed him three times in a vision. Both Jonah and Peter introduced salvation to the gentiles. It is why Peter was a son of the ministry of Jonah because, in this regard, they both took God's message to Gentile people.

The reason Jesus called Simon Peter "son of Jonah" was because of Peter's confession about who Jesus was. Jonah was the first to do it, and Peter did it also.

Therefore, when Peter spoke, "You are the Son of the living God," this caught Jesus's attention since this kind of profession only occurred once before, even then, uttering those earthly words moved a heavenly throne. Up to that time, Jesus had not been revealed in this manner yet, and that information was a mystery. By speaking this hidden truth, the Galilean fisherman instantly stamped his ticket to be considered part of an elite company.

No one catches Jesus by surprise, yet something abruptly caused Him to give Peter an intense stare. What was it? It was not "shock" that drew His attention to the fisherman, but the faith declaration that came from his heart. When Peter said Jesus was the Son of the living God, there was no lip service to fluff up the ego. Simon Cephas Peter meant what he said from his heart, and genuine faith gets Jesus' attention every time.

We can say all kinds of things which sound useful to those listening in this world, and it gives us a good front yet moves nothing. However, when we exhibit genuine faith, God comes back for that. That is also to say, Jesus comes back for an authentic faith; it gets His attention.

> *...when the Son of Man comes, will He really find faith on the earth?*
>
> Luke 18:8

Only one prophet had seen this deep secret before, and like Jonah before him, Peter had just pulled something out of heaven down to the earth, right in front of everyone.

Jonah was in the beten dag, or belly of the great fish, when he declared, "Salvation is of the Lord" (Jonah 2:9). Some have said this is the central verse of Scripture, just as some have said Peter's confession that Jesus is the "Son of the living God" is the central heartbeat of the church.

What Jonah revealed is that salvation comes from the Lord and only from Him, yet when we read it in the original language, a new understanding unveils itself. In Hebrew, the phrase reads as only two words: Yeshua Yehovah.

Yehovah is Hebrew for "the Lord," or Jehovah, in English, but look at the other word. It is yeshuah. Jesus is the English version of His name, but in Hebrew, it is Yeshua, which means "salvation." Jonah was a prophet, and he got a vision from heaven; he declared that Yeshua is of Yehovah, just as Peter proclaimed that Jesus was of the living God.

Both men made declarations central to the mystery of Christ.

That is not all the similarities between a fisherman and a prophet. Jonah and Peter had remarkably similar events in their lives, attesting to the fact Jesus gave Peter Jonah's prophetic mantle.

Jesus was familiar with the prophet Jonah, for though the son of Amittai lived eight hundred years before Jesus was born, the runaway prophet resided only three miles from Nazareth, where Jesus grew up, in a place called Gath-Hepher. Three miles was an easy walk for the young Messiah to visit the home of the local hero prophet.

Also, Jonah is one of just four prophets Jesus mentions in the Gospels and the only one to which He compares Himself in Matthew 12:40. Jesus knew Jonah very well because he was Jesus' hometown prophet.

So, when Jesus calls Peter a son of Jonah, it has implications of destiny. Read the list below to see how similar the lives of Peter and Jonah were.

Both Peter and Jonah:

- Made confessions of faith about Christ.
- Opened up salvation to the gentiles.
- Were called by the Word of the Lord.
- Had tempers.
- Rebuked the Lord (Jonah in Jonah 4:2; Peter in Matthew 16:22).
- Were fearful and ran away from or denied the Lord but later became bold to complete what the Lord had given them to do.
- Were connected with fish.
- Were connected with Joppa.

- Bravely got out of a boat during a fierce storm.
- Sank in the water.
- Nearly drowned.
- Called to the Lord when they were drowning.
- Were restored to their calling on a shore.
- Were saved by the Lord.
- Later went to the gentiles to preach.
- Preached boldly in a city (Jonah to Nineveh; Peter to Jerusalem).
- Preached incredible revivals.
- Had sullen attitudes after miracles, with which the Lord had to intervene.
- Finally, for both, the gates of hell could not overcome (Jonah 2:6; Matthew 16:18).

Therefore, when Jesus called Simon Peter, the "son of Jonah," it was because he would do similar things as Jonah. The Lord was calling Peter by his prophetic name, and I think He called Peter the son of Jonah because he held a special place in His heart. Both Peter and Jonah recorded the long-suffering of the Lord in their lives, so He must have loved them both.

Then it hit me, and I promptly understood why so many storms came into my life because Peter and Jonah both dealt with their tempests, too. When God called me Jonah, then I knew I was like them, and realized that I was experiencing the power of a name-calling God.

I remember, as a new believer, I told my mother I was about to go through a storm. If anyone asked me how I was aware of this, I could not have answered, but somehow, I knew. God gently revealed it to me, though I was not yet mature enough to understand how the Spirit moved in such matters. Still, the evidence was that my mother believed this came from God, but she warned, "Pray that whatever comes is financial because you can recover from that."

My storm came, and though it was not about money, I did recover. After that came another, with a similar one following that, and here I am writing in the midst of still another. All of this because I, too, have a Jonah calling.

The exciting part is that these storms ended neither Jonah nor Peter's life, for each of these men had yet to fulfill a godly purpose.

Realizing this, I accept that dealing with contrary winds are a portion of being selected.

I concluded that when the Lord called me "Jonah!", He was telling me that I was treasured and had a purpose.

We can only find our destiny in our heavenly name

So, the question hangs in the air, "Have we heard God called our second name?"

Brian Louis Perkins

10
God Will Make Our Name Great

> *I will make... your name great; and you shall be a blessing.*
>
> Genesis 12:2

God wants us to be great.

The disciples felt this greatness swelling up within them the more they hung around Jesus. Peter, an everyday fisherman, became such an outstanding speaker he wowed the teachers of the law, and they noted this was because he had spent time with the Messiah. His insightfulness belayed his rough Galilean appearance because he looked like an average working man, but how did he say these beautiful, deep things?

The smallest will become chief, and this is what happened to Peter. Compare him to Paul, who himself was taught by the keenest intellect of his day. Peter was not educated in man's religion, but only by the very words of God, yet Paul came to him for confirmation for fifteen days. Paul needed to make sure what he had learned from the Holy Spirit was what Peter had heard from Jesus. Paul, the trained Pharisee, desired to have his word confirmed by Peter, the common fisherman, before he would preach it.

Think about this, some consider Paul to have been one of the greatest intellects of history, but he, trained in the best teaching humanity had to offer in his day, wanted to confirm his revelation to a commoner before he would release it.

Here we observe how God made Peter the eye-catching pearl of his day, and this is what He wants to do for us. He has grandness in mind for us when we struggle to figure out the next thing to come. The very act of God calling our name cries out to greatness.

Jesus said if we want to be first or most celebrated in the kingdom, we must serve others. That is wisdom this world does not teach and a lesson which only comes from heaven.

We cannot fathom ourselves cloaked in dignity, yet God does. He says, do not run after our exaltation as the main thing, but strive to humble our hearts instead. We must work to minister to those around us.

The grandeur God intertwines in our spiritual name is in our call. We may be like the Lord in that we came to be a ransom for many through a sacrifice, and this world might never witness our majesty this side of eternity.

> *If any would come after Me, let him deny himself and take up his cross and follow Me.*
>
> Luke 9:23

In whatever assignment the Lord calls us to and names us for, we will have victory in Jesus. Many of us no longer seek this because we have given hope of overcoming even our daily existence, we would be satisfied with just surviving.

God built us for the impossible

The Beautiful Call: When God Reveals Our Name

When we get to the place where we look back on our lives, we will be astonished to see the awesome things God has done through us, and how He has led us in triumph. There is more to this life and the life to come than just existing in the mundane, every day. If we will only believe for the things which are too big for us, then we will watch God move on our behalf to give us a great name.

We will stare at overwhelming odds and say, "Lord, I can't do this," but He will whisper in our spirits, "When we face an impossibility, say to this thing, "I can, and God can, and it will be done."

If we have the faith of a mustard seed, we can say to this insurmountable mountain blocking our way, "Throw yourself into the sea, and get out of our way!" With that, unfeasibly tricky things will be removed out of our path. If we say, "I can," then we will; but if we say, "I can't," we will not succeed.

Do we realize that Moses climbed a mountain on the day he died when he was 120 years old? Some of us say we cannot walk around the block, and here Moses was rising to the top of a mountain peak on the last day of his life. What extraordinary thing will we be remembered for when we look over our life-course?

There are moments when we do not have a clue what or how to do anything. The Lord gave my wife a phrase concerning impossibilities when they present themselves against us. When we question how something is going to happen, because it is seemingly too hard for us to accomplish, He told her, "It is not about the 'how' but about the 'who.'" The only difference between 'how' and 'who' is how we arrange the letters, but the definitions produce different results.

As our results are controlled by rearranging letters, so are our victories come in the arrangement of our priorities. To be influential, we must believe God is greater than the impossibility set before us. Is it the problem that has an overcoming influence on us, or does God have more? An inspirational person will overcome the situation and not let the obstacle overtake them. Let us be that person.

When we view the Lord as more significant and more excellent than our problems, then our hindrances are smaller and inferior.

God gives prophetic dreams and hidden destinies contained in the name by which He calls us. He is the Name-Caller. Jesus walks around, speaking over us here and singing over us there;

then, the Lord declares our secret name, which heaven celebrates. Through this action, He activates those things planted in our souls from before our formation in our mother's wombs. He energizes that seed which up to now has lain dormant, merely waiting for the Lord to pass by.

His sweet call animates something deep down inside of us and lets us know that we have always been known and that our place is valued, and our mission is essential. It will change the world for someone if we will just let His voice quicken us to do what we were born to do.

Who knows what the next line will be? Who can say what the following step is? But if we listen to the beautiful call and review our accomplishments, we will see how much we achieved by the name which the Name Caller delivered to us.

Jesus came to make the way, but the Holy Spirit arrived to prepare us for the journey. The Lord is taking us somewhere grand, and God is maturing us so that we can enter greater things. He will give us a marvelous name because His name is above every name.

The Hebrew word for great is gadowl, and it appears 529 times in the Old Testament. Another term is rabh, which is employed 439 more times.

In the Greek, it is megas, used 195 times, and polys over 365 times. Over 1500 instances present the word great in Scripture, which leads us to something God has in mind for us. Polys was written 365 times, which is once for every day of the year.

Jesus will make our name well known, but only for His glory, not ours, because He has called us to His kingdom.

Yet when we hear our heavenly name, we will be affirmed not only in who we are but in what we are born to do. Our time is at hand.

The Third Call - Time

> *...there is a... time for every purpose under heaven:*
>
> Ecclesiastes 3:1

THE TIMES ARE A-CALLIN'!

God calls a "time" for us.

This section introduces some mind-bending concepts, and for that reason alone, apologies are offered like roses given with affection. A grand concept is about to unfold, and wisdom is required to work this out. Here is the main idea: God controls Time, using our seasons like tools in His hands. He shapes us with these instruments and causes us to mature so we can shine when "our time comes." He commands our past, future, and present, using time to fight for us and keep secrets hidden, which can only be unlocked at the "right time."

Dig in deep and realize:

Time is in God's hands

The Hebrew word moed is used for "an appointed time" and designates a particular moment when God meets with us. The Lord appoints our time and intersects with us at the crossroads of our lives, and therefore, He calls us at the right time to the right place. It is when He has chosen to do a great work, quite possibly a miracle.

Brian Louis Perkins

11
The Beautiful Gate

> *And a certain man, lame from his mother's womb, was carried, whom they laid daily at the gate of the temple, which is called Beautiful, to ask alms from those who entered the temple.*
>
> – Acts 3:2

W E SPEAK OF MIRACLES.

Peter came upon a man at the Beautiful Gate.

This lame person had been crippled from birth, but a wonder was about to happen in front of all the people because this was the crippled man's day.

The entrance called Beautiful can be translated as "the gateway of the right time." The Greek word used to describe the gateway is horaios, which can mean "fair, beautiful, or blooming," hence, the name the Beautiful (horaios) Gate. But this term can also be defined as "belonging to the right hour or season" or "ripe or mature." Is this not the importance of the horaios passage? When we have entered our opportune time and the moment is upon us, we produce our divine bloom. We become all we were meant to be, wrapped in beautified (horaios) destiny, and from this point, the Lord meets us as He accelerates us into our purposeful season, to accomplish that which we were born to do.

At the right time, we stand at the door of a beautiful call from the Lord, and our day is at hand. Precisely then, at the moedim, or appointed time, we walk onto the stage for the scene of our lifetime. When we are at the gate of the right time, the Lord changes our lives in an instant.

Think another way about this. A flower starts from a single seed, and yet, one day grows into maturity. It comes into its fullness, producing flowers of beauty inspiring the world and rekindling natural life. At its proper time, the plant is beautified. We will also reach our purpose and achieve our perfect place, which will inspire others to eternal life.

It reminds us of the Hebrew expression tov, which means "good." Moses used this term to describe God's reaction after creating the Universe. The Lord looked and declared that what He had made was tov, which is a word conveying that good is not a moral choice such as, "We did a good thing," or a preference, "That was a good meal." It infers that whatever was created was in its right place and doing what God made it to do, becoming superb. The Lord looked at the sun, the moon, and the stars, and surveyed how they were all in their place doing what He designed them to do; they were tov.

When something is tov, it is operating in its predesigned function. When something is accomplishing its purpose, it is beautified.

Jesus creates because He is the Word, but the Holy Spirit beautifies. Notice in Genesis 1:2 that it is the Spirit of God who is hovering, or brooding, over the waters.

In Job 26:13, God's Spirit is revealed as the person of the Trinity who garnishes creation.

By His Spirit, He adorned the heavens.

- Job 26:13

The Beautiful Call: When God Reveals Our Name

The Holy Spirit is the beautifier of nature. He makes the stars shine in their various glories and the plants to bloom or bear fruit. It is by the abiding work of the Holy Spirit in which we are brought to our fullness, our maturity, our destiny. When we move into where we are supposed to be and begin doing what we were made for, then we blossom. We become tov at the gateway of horaios or the right time. It is the Holy Spirit who beautifies His people in their season.

He has made everything beautiful in its time.

- Ecclesiastes 3:11

It is at the gate called Beautiful, where the disabled man was beautified by the miracle-working power of the Holy Spirit. He was lame, but that day was his to shine and blossom.

Peter said, "Silver and gold I do not have, but what I do have I give you: In the name of Jesus Christ of Nazareth, rise up and walk."

- Acts 3:6

The people watched with astonishment as this man jumped up and walked. He entered the temple with Peter and John, jumping and praising God. The Lord had caused him to shine at the gate named "beautiful."

The Beautiful Call is the right-time call

This man was born to praise God and bring glory to His name by being healed on that day; it was his fullness.

The news of this spread like wildfire, amazing everyone, and they gathered around Peter and John at the part of the temple named Solomon's Porch. There Peter preached, and five thousand men - many more including women and children - were added to the kingdom, even more than on the day of Pentecost.

The Beautiful Call: When God Reveals Our Name

We see this was a beautiful moment, as God called to the crowd, and they responded, becoming tov at the fullness of that moment. There were many beautiful calls at many gates.

Jesus raised a man from the dead who was the only offspring of a woman whose husband had long passed. All she had left in her world was her boy, but now he too had fallen.

> *And when He came near the gate of the city, behold, a dead man was being carried out, the only son of his mother; and she was a widow... Then He came and touched the open coffin, and those who carried him stood still. And He said, "Young man, I say to you, arise." So, he who was dead sat up and began to speak. And He presented him to his mother.*
>
> *- Luke 7:12, 14-15*

As God was calling Peter in Joppa to go to the gentiles, men were waiting for Peter at his entrance:

> *Now while Peter wondered within himself what this vision which he had seen meant, behold, the men who had been sent from Cornelius had made inquiry for Simon's house and stood before the gate.*
>
> — Acts 10:17

A broad doorway and a strait one presents itself to us on our journey. The wider door brings us to death, while the confined entryway's attraction is its beauty, calling to passersby with eternal life.

> *Enter by the narrow gate; for wide is the gate and broad is the way that leads to destruction, and there are many who go in by it. Because narrow is the gate and difficult is the way which leads to life, and there are few who find it.*
>
> — Matthew 7:13-14

God is looking to meet us at the gate, or door, of our next season with an open call, a promise of adornment to come into the fullness of our destiny, to bring us to the purpose we are to accomplish.

> *Two roads diverged in a wood, and I... took the one less traveled by, and that has made all the difference.*[11]

Listen for an appealing invitation at the beautiful gate because that is where God is calling us to our time.

Brian Louis Perkins

12
The Unpredictable Now

> *"...Our God is in heaven; He does whatever He pleases."*
>
> Psalm 115:3

W E WILL COME INTO OUR TIME.

And when we do, the enemy take stand against us. He confronts us at the door of our destiny. We label this a circumstance because we will just go around the mountain due to Lucifer's diversionary tactics instead of going through the gateway at our appointed time.

Satan hinders us from moving into our season by blocking or veering us off course, so that we cannot get ahead. We become entangled in a destructive cycle, meaning that the serpent has taken a stance against our destiny.

The Beautiful Call: When God Reveals Our Name

Do we notice the wordplay of circumstance and Serpent-stance? Something has been hidden there for a long time that is working against us.

The devil always tries to stop what God is doing on earth, so when he sees a heavenly outbreak, he erects an assignment to impede that godly action from manifesting or, at least, delay its effect. He attempts to maneuver us out of our opportunity. When it is our time, he seeks to push us into the wrong place so that we are out of sync with our purpose.

We must go to heaven's courts and plead for our time to be re-synced. Like Daylight Saving Time, we have to reset our clock, or we will miss out on opportunities. How many of us have been late to church or work because the time changed, and we did not fix our clocks? We need to know what time it is so we can react appropriately.

We have seen this on movies and television: they must prevent an explosion before the chance slips away, or a spy has to complete his mission before the adversary discovers what is happening. If the bomb goes off or an opponent finds out, things will change for the worse. However, if the device is stopped, or the mission completed in advance, matters will improve drastically.

God calls us to the most exciting assignments

He will reach out to us with a Holy Spirit unction or press us to move in the now.

For this reason, God maneuvers in such a manner as to catch the god of this world off guard. Satan does not understand the working of the Holy Spirit, nor can he predict His movements.

Like the Wind

The wind blows where it wishes, and you hear the sound of it, but cannot tell where it comes from or where it goes. So is everyone who is born of the Spirit.

- John 3:8

WE SETTLE FOR BEING DUST.

But we should be the wind.

Scripture tells us that the Holy Spirit moves like the wind and where He will go or what He will do, no one can predict.

John 3:8 are some of the most strategic words Jesus ever uttered on record, for here He is telling a teacher of Israel things the teacher should have already known but did not: The Holy Spirit's nature is seen in the wind. The word used for wind is pneuma, which can mean "wind," "spirit," or "ghost," or the Holy

Spirit. The wind is nature's perfect example to illustrate the Holy Spirit because it shows how unpredictable He is and how difficult the task becomes for the enemy to figure Him out.

In effect, Jesus was saying, "Look at the wind. You can see how the current goes wherever it pleases." We could imagine Jesus implying "and no one can stop that wind either." In this example, the wind acts like a person going where they want. We can catch on to this behavior because sound is the wind's call.

Everyone knows beautiful descriptions written about the noise of the wind which moves mysteriously through trees and sweeps gracefully over grasslands. The breeze whispers one way through the needles of an Australian pine tree, differently through the fronds of a coconut palm, and still another way echoing through a canyon bringing along with it the pitch of whistles, howls, or gusts. At other times, a refreshing breath is how the wind presents itself, yet either way, we detect its voice. From the sound "mood," whether a lapping airflow or one whipped up into a fury, we notice what the wind is about to do.

Jesus indicates that if we will harken to the tone of the wind we will pick up on its mood, which also shows us that we will likewise pick up the mood of the Holy Spirit as He moves among us. We will learn to know what the Holy Spirit's disposition is or what He is planning to do simply by listening to His vocal inflection. The Holy Spirit forms sounds we can detect, for the beautiful call comes through Him.

> *The Spirit Himself makes intercession for us* ***with groanings which cannot be uttered.***
>
> - Romans 8:26, emphasis added

The Holy Spirit makes guttural reactions with sounds. In one version, the verse reads, "with groanings too deep for words." Wailings are sounds without dialog, and this is how the Holy Spirit calls to us as He goes by.

When Jesus says, "The wind goes wherever it wants, and you will discover its sound," He is confirming to us that the Holy Spirit has a purpose in mind and that as He passes by, He is calling with sounds too deep for words. Those who will become wise to the effect will learn His passions.

God is inviting us to act when He makes the "sound" to heal, to meet a personal need for another person, to speak a word of encouragement. He wants us to move to help the widow and the orphan, to give light to those in darkness, to bring salvation to those who need to be saved. The Holy Spirit is making the call for us to partner with Him to usher in the agenda of heaven upon the earth.

Jesus also tells us of another characteristic of the wind: its unpredictability. "But [we] cannot tell where it comes from and where it goes." The Holy Spirit is like this. We are not able to tell where He is going or what He is going to do next, and this is His uncontrollable nature.

Satan hates not being able to predict what is coming next, for if he knew that, he would try to contain the outbreak. This super-nature of the Spirit of God is what upsets the devil's applecart. He is unable to stop God's will because he does not know what the Holy Ghost will do next.

He may prepare for the stopping of a godly breakthrough in progress over here. Still, because a Sunday school teacher heard the Spirit's unpredictable call to share the gospel with a shoe salesman, revival broke out across the world. Unable to expect what the Spirit will do next keeps Satan's hands full.

The Holy Spirit, like the wind, working in mysterious ways.

He makes calls when He moves by those of us who will partner with the miracle He desires to perform.

When the Spirit runs by us, and we feel this gentle pressure of His nudge to say or do something, we know it because sometimes we fight it. We find out the mood of His sound as He calls out to us, and then we will know what to.

Whatever it is, it will be something unpredictable.

Catching the Devil
Off Guard

THIS IS THE UNPREDICTABLE NOW.

Many times, we back down from that God moment - the unction of the Holy Spirit to act now - because we fear embarrassment or adverse reaction from those around us. But if we would respond to the Holy Spirit's prompting, we would unleash some change for the better.

Are we responding to the unpredictable call from the Holy Spirit? He wants to surprise the adversary if we would only follow His urging, but most of the time, we back down.

If we do something for God this world expects, such as giving to the poor, no one is astonished by the act because people do it all the time. However, if we do what is unanticipated, they are shocked - like feeding five thousand people with two fish and five loaves. It still fed the poor, but this was accomplished in such a remarkable way that its fame spread far and wide, and many people traveled to see who did this marvelous deed. The Spirit of God understands what will catch the devil off guard, and He wants to do this so reform can enter the physical realm from heaven. It puts our foe at a significant disadvantage when he cannot predict God's next step. The devil could be in the wrong place at the wrong time before he could build up any resistance to the move of God until it was too late. This is why it is critical to follow the Holy Spirit's lead.

The Spirit of God also knows what astonishes people to turn their hearts to Jesus. The Son of God was the most astounding person ever to set foot in this world, and those unusual things He did are recorded in Scripture. Everywhere He went, the people were surprised at what He said and did.

> *And so, it was, when Jesus had ended these sayings, that the people were astounded by His teaching.*
>
> *- Matthew 7:28*

And straightway, the damsel arose and walked; for she was of the age of twelve years. And they were astonished by a great astonishment.

Mark 5:42 KJV

When He had come to His own country, He taught them in their synagogue, so that they were astonished and said, "Where did this Man get this wisdom and these mighty works?"

Matthew 13:54

Jesus was always ahead of anything that His opponent was doing, keeping Satan on his heels whenever He spoke or did something. This is how the Holy Spirit is, and the different thing about all of this is that we are to be like Him.

Look at the last part of what Jesus delivered to us about the wind in John 3:8. He said that the wind goes wherever it desires, and no one can predict if it is coming or going.

"So, it is with everyone born of the Spirit."

That means we are to go, do, and say like the wind - or as the Holy Spirit moves - because we hear His sound. It also gives rise to the idea that we are agents of the unpredictable now. Like Jesus, we can be a step in front of the serpent, pushing him off-kilter by what we say or do because we are listening to the untraceable call of the Holy Spirit.

It takes an unpredictable now to break the enemy's strategy against us. If he has engineered a blockade to keep us from our breakthrough, then an "unpredictable now" move of the Holy Spirit frustrates his plans. Think about this. Lucifer would be the one frustrated instead of us. We need to only listen to the beautiful appeal of the Spirit of God.

When the Spirit's plea is pressing us into action, He is about to unloose transformation on the earth. When He emphasizes an action or a word from us, and we know God longs to do something, He is about to thwart an obstruction of justice in a situation.

His passion is to interact upon a scene to bring freedom, betterment, and miracle-working power, which will bear down upon an evil serpent-stance. He wants to destroy the barrier defeating us from possessing our time. When God persuades us to jump into the fray, and we obey, it will make the accuser go away for a season.

God is compelling us to become like Him: "Unstoppable" in an unpredictable *now*.

13
Calling Our Future and Past into Our Now

How good is a timely word!

– Proverbs 15:23 NIV

Time will tell.

Physicists say time is like an arrow that moves in only one direction, but we all have instances which tell us something weird is happening with the time around us: déjà vu moments, dreams, and flashes where time appears to stand still or even quicken.

The older we get, the more we feel as if time seems to go by faster every year, like we are traveling toward a waterfall.

In this manner, the passage of time is mysterious, but the times are in God's hands. The Lord lives outside of its effects in a place we call eternity, a realm where days, hours, and minutes are captured and held motionless. Eons do not drag on or speed up there since no measurement of time exists where God is. In eternity, time is observed as a robust story. It is why God can see our beginning from our ending because our stories are laid out before Him like a scroll unwound for his viewing.

Eternity has no constraint, but time does, and therein lies the difference. We often say, "Time's up!" or "We are running out of time," to convey its cutoff point and when Scripture decrees that a man's life is but a wisp of vapor (James 4:14), this speaks of a boundary assigned to our lifespan.

When Albert Einstein discovered the theory of relativity, his ideas involved an understanding concerning time. One of the great thoughts which came out of his work was the connection of space and time. They were part of an interwoven fabric that we now call the space-time continuum.

From his ideas, the cosmos itself became viewed as a "fabric" intimately tied to time, and Einstein theorized an expansion of it. This idea alone gave us two key concepts: the universe and time are like a cloth, and like any material, stretching turned out to be a distinct possibility. When a fabric is pulled in one direction, the other side is affected as well. It means that whatever affects space also affects time.

This concept has many implications. Seventeen times Scripture declares creation was pulled like a curtain, or a tent, by the hand of God. Whenever the celestial medium is stretched, it forces a change in time as well, according to Einstein's assumptions. Being elastic, time folds like a rubber band in God's hands.

Though science says time travels like an arrow, always forward and never in reverse, schools of thought exist for time travel in the scientific community. However, though most of these concepts are in found in fiction, the concepts still survive.

With God, time becomes a powerfully controlled commodity.

The Beautiful Call: When God Reveals Our Name

Scripture often shows God's mastery over it, for He can make time stand still just as He did for Joshua, and likewise, He can also accelerate its flow.

When God curbs time, we notice immediately saying that a moment has become "timeless." We write songs about it. Even in our moviemaking, we slow down important scenes, bringing added impact to the storyline because changing the timing gets our attention. We describe time slowing down in harrowing situations like this example, "My life flashed before my eyes." Our entire life rolls before us in a vision, arrayed in wonder, all within the framework of a few seconds, and this is like the myrtle tree story I told earlier. Some say, "Time stood still," when they encounter an angelic being.

As God enters the room, eternity rushes in, too, and where the infinite is, time proves to be inoperative.

God used the almond branch for the first menorah design, and when He did this, He was saying something about time. Why we may ask? Because the almond tree is known for budding and producing its fruit overnight, even though the previous day, its branches looked as though they were only dead sticks. What God is showing us is that when He accelerates time, He also matures the produce, and causes what once took years to grow, to ripen in mere months, days, or even instantaneously. Remember, when the fruit appears, it has reached the end stage of its purpose, which was to render a harvest for the season. Becoming ripe or mature, it becomes horaios – beautiful - for God makes everything beautiful in its time. Accelerating time quickly ripens the yield we produce.

Stretching and Inserting Time

*And this is the sign to you from the Lord, that the Lord will do this thing which He has spoken: Behold, I will bring the shadow on the sundial, which has gone down with the sun on the sundial of Ahaz, **ten degrees backward.**" So, the sun returned ten degrees on the dial by which it had gone down.*

Isaiah 38:7-8, emphasis added

T IME IS A FUNNY THING.

God can stretch time like a rubber band to make its passage slow down or hurry, but He can also insert time. Do we realize that in His hands, time is a thing for Him to use, like an instrument designed to accomplish a task? He can stop time as He did with Moses's protege, having the sun stand still for a whole day (Joshua 10:13), and at other times He can accelerate it.

We read that Hezekiah asked God to perform a sign that he would be healed from his sickness, and Isaiah was the prophet who inquired of the Lord for him. Isaiah gave Hezekiah a choice of signs, both of which involved time: will God move time forward or back it up? The sickly king chose to have more time, so he asked to have time's shadow back up. It presented him with the gift of having more time added to his life (2 Kings 20:10).

Another example we rarely think of where God directed time to achieve His purposes is when God inserted time for mercy. It was such a surprise which no one, not even the spiritual rulers of this world, foresaw. It was a shock when condemnation was deferred. As time winds down from the beginning to the end of the world, a fearful ruling before a holy God is assumed. People could feel that they were counting down to a fearful judgment. Nevertheless, this verdict is not in what God delights; He loves mercy (1 Peter 1:3), so He paused it when Jesus showed up on the scene.

While everyone anticipated punishment, He made time for graciousness, catching all off guard. Jesus came personally to stop judgment time and squeeze in an era of grace. See what even the demons of hell, who operated in the earth, said as they saw Jesus show up on the scene.

> *And suddenly they cried out, saying, "What have we to do with You, Jesus, You Son of God? Have You come here to torment us before the time?"*
>
> Matthew 8:29

The rule of darkness expects to be judged for their rebellion, but when Jesus appeared before them, they were surprised. They had not expected Him to come for them before "the time" of the verdict. However, Jesus's unpredictable appearance was devised by the Father for another purpose than to speed up the sentencing; it was to freeze time altogether. It was evidenced by Time being split on our calendar. We separate our calendar from B.C. (Before Christ) to A.D. (Anno Domingo), the Year of Our Lord. When Jesus set foot in this world, time changed, and this will happen again when He returns in Millennial time. Every time the Lord comes to the earth, the ages change.

When devils see Jesus, they become agitated because the Son of Glory represents judgment to them. Just talk about Jesus in the public square and watch the fireworks. Enemies of Christianity love to restrain Jesus and the mention of His name because at the name of Jesus, every knee will bow, and every tongue confess that Jesus is Lord. They know what it means: they will be tried for their wicked deeds.

The Lake of Fire was not created for people, but for those fallen angels and evil spirits who rebelled from God's perfection. Jesus knows this and is the very reason He came because He stated clearly in.

> *For God did not send His Son into the world to condemn the world, but that the world through Him might be saved.*
>
> John 3:17

Humanity will be given an opportunity for mercy and grace if they respond to His beautiful invitation. It is why we have a church at all: to make the Beautiful Call to humanity.

The church's role in this world is to call, "Mercy! Mercy! A time of Mercy is upon us!" for those who will receive it. We have been redeemed, from destruction ourselves, and now are propelled into the benefits of God; and all He asks is for us to tell others this Good News.

Jesus stopped judgment time and inserted a season of Grace and Mercy.

It will give the human race an extension to decide in favor of Jesus as Savior or Sentencer. We are compelled to choose Him as Savior.

The Lord stopped condemnation and injected an age for the church which no one saw coming, though it was foretold in Scripture (Daniel 9:25-26). This age was a hidden mystery

(Romans 16:25). God gave 490 years (or poetically, 70 "weeks" of years; aka 70 x 7 = 490) to deal with Israel, where a week of years is seven years. From the building of Jerusalem to the restoration of the kingdom, 490 years would pass, yet during a specific point in this countdown, God would do this radical thing - He gave us more time.

At the 483 years' mark, the clock for Israel stopped (not that God was done dealing with Israel, for He is not). At the end of 483 years, counting from the building of Jerusalem to when the Messiah was cut off. This cutting off was when they crucified Jesus.

70 "Weeks" of Years - 70 x7 = 490

		approx 2000 years Inserted into the 490	
	Crucifixion	CHURCH AGE	Final 7 years
1	483	INSERTED	490

ISRAEL's TIMELINE

> *Know therefore and understand, that from the going forth of the command to restore and build Jerusalem until Messiah the Prince, there shall be seven weeks and sixty-two weeks... And after the sixty-two weeks, Messiah shall be cut off.*
>
> - Daniel 9:25-26

Seven "weeks" of years are 49 years, while 62 "weeks" of years are 434 years; add 49 to 434, and we get 483 years from Jerusalem's start to the death of Christ. It stopped the time of the 490-year cycle, and as Israel is always the apple of God's eye, making it irreplaceable in the plans of God, this still left one week of years to complete when the Lord finalizes His affairs with Israel. The remaining seven years is recognized as the time of Jacob's trouble, and during this last week of years, God will save all Israel.

But here is the point: There was a plan to introduce time for mercy, which became the Age of Grace. The Lord administered this era through the church. And after grace has run its course (at the fulfillment of the Gentiles), the countdown sentencing will resume.

God stopped judgment time to imbed grace for those on the earth - or peace and goodwill, as announced at the birth of Jesus. This introduction of mercy and grace is the revelation, and it is why the Bible declares, "now is the day of salvation" (2 Corinthians 6:2).

The Lord spliced in some time so we could be reconciled to a loving Father, and He held back the hand of judgment because of His cross and resurrection. As Jesus declared, "I did not come to judge the world" (John 12:47), but He came to reconcile it - as we have also been called to do. God creates time for that. We are to be busy about the Father's business "reconciling" in the inserted age of Grace until it ends. When this mercy-time concludes, the countdown will pick up where it left off, completing the final seven years of Israel's timeline.

The bigger idea here is that God can inject a season anywhere at any "time." Not only can He implant it in a timeline, but He can also make it. If we need Him, God can literally make time for us just as He has made time for mercy. He can make time out of thin air to spend with us, and He can produce an appointed time to call us as well.

Brian Louis Perkins

Ahead of Our Time

> *By faith Abraham... waited for the city which has foundations, whose builder and maker is God.*
>
> Hebrews 11:8-10

ABRAHAM SAW A TIMELESS CITY.

He glimpsed the glorious place "a far off," which was a way to say he had a prophetic vision peering into the hereafter where an eternal Jerusalem of the future would become the "now."

History is the recounting of the past in our now. We are His story in the making, so He can pull things we learned in former times to improve our "now" with a better choice gained from prior experience.

Similarly, our "time to come" structures this way as well for we can learn from the "future" for our "now."

> *For now, we see through a glass, dimly, but then face to face. Now I know in part, but then I shall know just as I also am known.*
>
> - 1 Corinthians 13:12, emphasis added

Paul says he knows "now," but in the "sweet by and by," he would know just as he was already known. This phrase uses the same term three times as we read in modern Bibles, given the last was a variant of know (known). But something indeed fell out of the English translation because the same word was not chosen when penned using the original language. From the Greek, it would look like this: "Now I ginosko, but then . . . shall I epiginōskō . . . as I am epiginōskō."

The expression for "know" changes from ginosko, which infers "to know," to epiginōskō, or "to know." The prefix epi makes all the difference.

Epi means something specific, and we will come to that shortly, but first, we must grasp ginosko. It proposes to know something from what we have learned, to "come to understand, or to learn" something from our past. In Thayer's Greek-English Lexicon, it states two unique traits of this word: "the truth of the promise" and "was readily understood from what had preceded."[12]

Both had a time element to them. The "truth of the promise" was understood as something promised in the past. We were waiting for it to be fulfilled in a future time. It means to learn of a future thing from something in the past, such as a prophecy or a promise. It was the learning of the future, but never from the future and always pointing to some past thing.

The emphasis of this word was that our knowledge came from what was behind us. We learned it from paths already traveled, never from a future which lay before us. It was why it was always said that if we fail to learn from our history, we will make the same mistakes we did before. Naturally, we learn from behind, never in front, or the future, inferring that we were always "behind" in our learning while we exist in this world, but Paul was letting us key in on something mind-boggling. He introduced a new word, actually a prefix of a word, that would alter history and the future alike. That authoritative little prefix was "epi."

Epi changes the meaning of ginosko to something else, but what? Epi was a word that had connotations of "above, after, beyond, further, over, toward." Paul was communicating that the learning, which was behind, at some point, switches to a forward position. It moves "after, further, or toward," or to "a higher position" as in "above, over, or beyond." Our learning shifts from behind to in front of and over us, not behind and under us. Our knowledge will come from beyond and not behind us.

We can learn from both or all directions.

God not only enables us to not only learn from our past but also our future.

**If we understood
what God is able to do with time,
we would be astonished.**

From time itself, we can receive help either from what we have learned in the past, or been prayed over, but we can also receive aid from foundations laid, or what had been prophesied over us in the past. However, we can get help from future learning, advanced revelation, dreams, or our inheritance already stored up for us from before the foundation of the world in heaven's storehouse.

It may be a problematic revelation for some of us because of what we accept about time. We have been trained from the viewpoint of the world, so time means a specific thing to us. I remember how I shook my head when this revelation came to me, but "in no time at all," it began to make sense. Then everything fell into place.

Prophets discerned this and would indiscriminately call things from the past or the future as the Spirit gave them the leading. We must train ourselves to be fluent with ideas from a heavenly viewpoint, and when we do, these concepts open up to us. God controls time, and that means something, for time itself becomes a powerful tool in God's hands.

The Beautiful Call: When God Reveals Our Name

Now Is Our Time

Time heals all wounds.

The reason we are talking about stretching, inserting, and making time is that from this action, God draws things from our past and future, bringing them into our now.

God pulls things from our ancient paths to sync with our now, which could be something as prayers offered by family members or prophetic words given over us. Perhaps, there is an appeal our mother prayed with the Lord before she passed away, yet the plea remains bottled up in heaven on the unanswered shelf near the Father's throne. It can also be a lineage that is pulled into our now, as when Jesus was called the Son of David, connecting Him to the line of kings that began under the man after God's own heart, giving Him a preferred heritage of authority to do what He did. God can go into the past and pull a resource into our now when needed most.

Things are set aside for us by our benefactors. They will be discharged at certain stages, encoded for us to have at the appropriate time.

Prayers and prophecies are laid up in the heavenlies waiting for the right time to be released. As we reach our critical time, heaven positions these resources, set up for us in our past, to be announced into our now. Our power to win the day has been hidden in our history all this time, safe from thieves' touch, until it was ready to utilize for our victory.

Elisha secured the mantle of the recently departed Elijah when he walked to the Jordan River with it in hand. He said, "Where is the God of Elijah?" With this, he was asking for the thing from his past experience to come into his present, by also striking his cloak to the water. The past met the now, and the water parted, just as it did for Elijah.

God can move things from our coming prospects into our now. He can unfold our future so we can grasp it during our current time.

We think poorly of the prodigal son. He begged for an early inheritance, and he becomes a rather disappointing figure in the story. But after consideration, we realize that it was not in the asking for money which makes us look down on him but in the haphazard way in which he spent it. Still, the first part of his request shows us that we can pull things from another place of resource to pull it down into our sphere of need, which is the here and now. That inheritance was available, and he tapped into it.

John the Baptist preached that the kingdom of heaven was coming.

> *About this time, John the Baptist appeared, preaching... "Repent, because the kingdom of heaven is near!"*
>
> — Matthew 3:1-2 ISV

Then Jesus announced it had come:

> *Behold, the kingdom of God is within you.*
>
> — Luke 17:21 KJV

The Beautiful Call: When God Reveals Our Name

Jesus took something from the past - John's proclamation - and pulled that into the now. "Forget not all His benefits," the psalmist says, and this can apply to the kingdom of heaven, for its advantages are unlimited and timeless. They apply anywhere, heaven or earth, at any time, and even apply inside or outside of time. They can be used everywhere.

Sometimes we cannot get to our future without grabbing hold of what preceded us. We may have to "go back" and fix something in our past before anything forward becomes an option for us. It is where God helps us because He can go into our historical records and cleanse a generational curse from a household line or erase an iniquity where there is no more precedent for working against us in our present. He can heal our "now" by moving back to a time when our family brought in sin, and as we repent in our now, He can go back to correct things in our timeline:

> *I will go before (paniym) thee, and make the crooked places straight...*
>
> Isaiah 45:2 KJV

The word before in Hebrew used here in Isaiah 45:2 is paniym, and one of its meanings is "a before time." He is saying that he can go to "a before time," a paniym, and make the uneven ways even and passable. God can fix our lineage, heal our history, and hide resources there that the devil cannot touch.

God is in eternity and can "step into" time at any point. He can go into our past from a prayer from our parents, or a prophetic word given from years ago, for example, and pull it into our now. He can repair the crooked way and put a foothold into our hereafter. The Lord can take our inheritance, or things from our heavenly storehouse, to bring into our present situation.

God is a God of the now.

Now is the day of salvation. It is never too late to pray. God can take prayers from the past or future and, by eternity's connection into all eras of time, make them of effect in our now.

It is not an invitation to miss any "time." It is for an appointed time for us to be in the right place at the right time, and if we move when the time is ripe, we will end up having the time of our lives. God is always on time because He can make time.

Time is a tool in God's hands

The times are a-callin', so watch Time work wonders in us for we are about to be revealed as something this world has never seen before.

Brian Louis Perkins

The Final Call - Revelation

Brian Louis Perkins

14

Call of the Beautifier

For the Lord... will beautify [adorn] the [meek] with salvation.

— Psalm 149:4

Now the earth was formless and empty, darkness was over the surface of the deep, and the Spirit of God was hovering over the waters.

— Genesis 1:2 NIV

FEW HAVE THOUGHT ABOUT THIS:

There exists a strong connection between the Holy Spirit and beauty. Since the time of the early Christian fathers, this idea has been found in their writings. We also understand it because our spirit testifies to the fact, but we do not know all the reasons why except that it just seems right. Therefore, the question lingers, "How is making something decorative tied to the Holy Spirit?"

One reason is that in this work of grandeur He does, there is something about it to do with His character; He embodies every aspect of splendor. One of His roles is to beautify creation.

When God called the universe into being, He spoke a word to accomplish this, and we know that word was, and is, Jesus. However, creation was not completed until the Ruach ha'Kodesh (Hebrew for Holy Spirit) did His work. Though the Father conceived the idea, and Jesus announced its essence, the Spirit of God created its "final" form. His Spirit beautified nature.

God is a spirit who transcends gender. He allows such descriptions for the physical world to help us relate to Him as Father, or the Son, of God. One of the concepts lost by translation of Hebrew into English is the gender of the Ruach ha'Kodesh, or the Holy Spirit, as a feminine term.

When we see the title, Holy Trinity, we rightly think of three as one, but generally of three male Persons as one God.

Another way to think of this is that the Trinity is a Holy Family, consisting of a Father, Mother, and a Child. We have no problem within our limited framework grasping that many persons can be one family, but we struggle with the three-in-one concept for God. Still, it is relatively easy to consider a household unit.

If we can accept this, it may help us understand that the Holy Spirit embodies characteristics generally found in mothers. Anyone who has a "Mom" knows how mothering moms can be. She hovers over us the way the Holy Ghost hovered over the waters. Mothers give birth and are more concerned with making things lovely, just as the Spirit of God does. The concept is easy for us to work with, that of a Holy Family.

Yet, I am Gentile and have been well-trained to call the Holy Spirit masculine, and I think that is correct also because, again, God is greater than gender. Once I complete this feminine explanation, I will refer to the Holy Ghost as "He" the rest of the way, but, first, a few more thoughts on the subject.

Consider where the roles of male and female come from if not God Himself? The Lord contains the elements of both genders, for He made the structure of a family, i.e., "male and female He created them" (Genesis 1:27). It is also generally accepted on a scholarly level that another term for God, El Shaddai, presents the feminine nature of God.

The point of this is not a kind of gender confusion but rather to understand God created both genders, and this male and female framework had to come from somewhere. He took of Himself and incorporated His characteristics in us, with masculine and feminine traits in the male and female versions of humanity, respectively.

If we are mature, we understand that God is above genderization, but His qualities were displayed in us who are fashioned in His image. The appreciation of beauty, adorning, hovering, brooding, and mothering all come from the Holy Spirit.

We catch the story of creation in Genesis 1:2.

And the Spirit of God moved upon the face of the waters.

When everything was in place, and Jesus had formed the earth, the Holy Spirit configured the final work. He put the icing on the cake. He made its final form.

Now think about this: a breath is required to carry out a command. As words fly upon the wind to be heard, so does it take a breath to transport speech. It means that words and breathing work in unison to bring something forth, so it only makes sense that Jesus (the speaker) and the Spirit (the breather) would labor hand in hand when speech was put into action to create. The Word forms, and the Spirit beautifies. I would rather say, the Word composes, and the Spirit sings since Jewish tradition holds that creation was sung into being.

Interestingly, the expression used for the Spirit of God moving confers "to brood or flutter," even "to shake." The implication concerns a mother bird who broods over her eggs for them to hatch; she flutters and shakes on them, brooding over them to emerge. It is what the Holy Spirit did upon the waters - He brooded like a mother bird, working to develop things in creation because He is the beautifier.

When God made the world, darkness ruled the void, but the Holy Spirit covered everything because He wanted to spark life into the darkness. He was about to bring color, ripeness, and glorious appeal.

When the Holy Spirit worked, He was getting ready to decorate with life, alluring variations, and brilliant hues. He illustrated our world, like an artist splashes a blank canvas. And this is another way in which to think of the Ruach ha'Kodesh: as an artist.

When real art is performed, we are taking on the nature of the Artiste, becoming like Him.

Below are some famous quotes about artists and their expressions of beauty.

Art is a collaboration between God and the artist, and the less the artist does the better.

-Andre Gilde

"In art, what we want is the certainty that one spark of original genius shall not be extinguished."

– Mary Cassatt

"Everybody born, comes from the Creator trailing wisps of glory. We come from the Creator with creativity. I think that each one of us is born with [it]."

– Maya Angelou

"It is wise to learn; it is God-like to create."

– John Saxe

The Beautiful Call: When God Reveals Our Name

Why is the world so full of fantastic variety? Because the Holy Spirit fashioned it that way. He painted upon the open sky and decorated the forest canopy beneath, He adorned wild beasts with agility, fur, and strength, and ornated tiny insects with crowns and colors. He layered nature with scenes solely designed to birth inspirations and images to witness soul-affirming truths. It is the art of the Holy Spirit which illustrates our world, and it was His personal masterpiece. Intertwined right in the fabric of Creation, He sewed in it a heartbeat all its own. Those who recognize this expression are drawn to nature's wonders because they pull our gaze up and beyond, telling us that Someone more significant than ourselves exists out there.

The Spirit of God chiseled mountains, carved out seas, and filled riverbeds. He sequined starfish under ocean waves and veneered birds nesting among clouds. Upon the ends of branches, He laid ornaments of flowers and underneath the earth, He poured gold and silver into its veins. My thought is the Holy Spirit was having immense pleasure in what He was doing, running around in a marvelous frenzy, painting, decorating, and telling stories within His artistry, some obvious and some locked, only to be revealed at the due time. To be sure, He was having fun.

The joy of Christmas preparation is putting up the tree. Think of Jesus making the tree, putting it into place so it would stand, but the Holy Spirit is the One donning the decorations. Let that sink in. Creation was the tree, and the Holy Spirit was the One who was honored to put all the ornaments and lights in their place.

If the Holy Spirit had not brooded over the waters and introduced colors and variety, we would have never known art, music, or natural elegance. We only know of these things because He "moved" upon the surface of the earth, decorating and adorning.

> *By His Spirit, He adorned the heavens.*
>
> *- Job 26:13*

The Holy Spirit is the One who delivered an appreciation of beauty that we see in an imaginative creation. Both colors and flowers are unnecessary for life, and is this not wondrous to think about? The world did not need blooms to fertilize new plants. It just as easily might come from some other part of the flora - may be the stem or leaf - but the blossom is where the Spirit of God chose to have fertilization reside. How beautiful an act He performed when He decided new life would be birthed from the most attractive portion, for the bees come there to gather the nectar of life. It became the lovely dance of renewal projected upon the canvas of nature.

Here is a concept only the Holy Spirit can conceive: New life replenished out of loveliness. It did not come from the roots, or the supporting stalk, but from the fragile flower where the seeds of new birth were placed. And He did this with flair and charisma, for we are attracted to His beautiful call. If all plants brought forth a green fruit, never using colors varying from its origin, we could still survive, but oh how that beauty makes life worthwhile. How many times have we sat upon a shore or a mountain and experienced a glorious sunset? It was here the Holy Spirit saddles up alongside and whispers to us, "So you like it, huh?" and we can barely respond under the weight of glory, "Oh…yes…" as our voice trails off with the wonder of it all.

There is a need for beauty, but not everyone sees it. A certain man has many crabapple trees flowering on his land each spring. They are the most beautiful ones anyone could ever hope to see, like a dreamy Hollywood movie set, yet he complains every year they only give him blossoms and never food. They are not useful to him, because he is forced to pick up what falls after their season is over since he is not looking for beauty but something to eat.

Yet, there exist ornamental orchards all over the earth. Why is that, especially if they serve no purpose? If there exists no need for beauty, then why do we have any ornate, non-fruit bearing plants at all? The motive behind creating these "non-useful" expressions of loveliness is that they call our attention to the masterful workings of the Holy Spirit. They are displayed as purposeful reminders that His majestic efforts were to make all things beautiful.

The Beautiful Call: When God Reveals Our Name

He has made everything beautiful in its time.

- Ecclesiastes 3:11

We would have had a more Spartan kind of living arrangement, if not for the Holy Spirit. By the joy He breathed in this world, beauty is allowed to thrive. Some plants' glory belongs within their aromas; others are lovely to look upon, while still others' have a grace which is in the great taste of their fruit. It was His beautiful call.

The Spirit adorns, decorates, beautifies, colors, and creates variety. Yet even produce is beautified, for a green tree can generate a red apple, a yellow banana, or an orange tangerine just as much as a green plant can bring forth a white bloom, a purple flower, or a pink rose. Why was this necessary unless the Spirit of God was making a statement to us about artistry?

The Holy Spirit's work of beautifying could be considered a subset of the broader category of ordering.40

The layer of beauty we see all around us suggests that Jesus laid the earth's foundation, but the Holy Spirit gave its completion. Our globe exploded with life. The world became this eruption of hues and variety, in all manner of plants and animals. Evolutionists are baffled by this sudden appearance of everything to the point they had to invent a term for it, which they now call "The Cambrian Explosion." They cannot explain why all plant and animal life suddenly came upon the scene together, yet they will not deny that it did.

The Cambrian explosion [was an event] when most major animal phyla appeared in the fossil record. Almost all present animal phyla appeared during this period.41

Amid this timeframe, all varieties of life resembled what they do today. Structure and variation burst on the scene, as if it all walked on the stage together, along with all of its differences and colors. Beauty erupted on the face of the earth with no explanation, and science cannot tell us why; it can only say that it happened all at once.

Powerfully, this shouts out proof within the scientific account of the work the Holy Spirit did in Genesis 1. In the Bible, it describes His actions as hovering, which caused life to flourish in diverse splendor everywhere. He birthed beauty in the world.

The Beautiful Call: When God Reveals Our Name

It was made especially the Holy Spirit's work to bring the world to its beauty and perfection out of the chaos, for the beauty of the world is a communication of God's beauty. The Holy Spirit is the harmony and excellency and beauty of the Deity . . . Therefore, it was his work to communicate beauty and harmony to the world, and so we read that it was he that moved upon the face of the waters.42

It did not end there, however, for He is the beautifier of all creation, including the stars. Yet among all of His works, this planet is unique; we have not found one evidential shred of life any other place, let alone anything near as full of life as our own. The earth is a world supporting 8.7 million different life forms.43 Atheist science confirms the variety of life here, but in the same breath, it tells us that our world is not extraordinary. It is almost insanity to consider what they are saying; what they are teaching us is like someone setting a beautiful plate on the table but having rotting food setting upon it.

This denial of the obvious is the motive why there is such a furious hunt for 'Earth-like' planets these days because they are desperate to undercut the claim that the earth is unique and favored by God.

No other place is adorned as our world, and, as has been said before, we are a jewel set in space. They will find no place like earth because only this place was favored to beautify since the Holy Spirit brooded here.

The Spirit of God is unlimited, meaning He not only broods over creation but does this also for us as He is the beautifier of the human soul. It is the work of the Spirit of God in a person. He adorns us as much as He did creation, and it also has something to do with divine glory.

The help of our countenance is from the Lord and His Spirit. God wants to restore everything to its original purpose, making it tov, or good. He will do this in the world now and for the world to come.

During the Rapture, when we put on immortality and have beautified bodies without flaws, everything about the glorified body will be exquisite. We will exist as the most beautiful people ever seen, a whole race of glorious ones. David, being a prophet, saw them and called them "the excellent ones":

The Beautiful Call: When God Reveals Our Name

As for the saints... "They are the excellent ones, in whom is all my delight."

- Psalm 16:3 ESV

But while we are here, in our lower state, we can still see the effects of being beautified.

You send forth Your Spirit... and You renew the face of the earth.

- Psalm 104:30

The Holy Spirit beautifies the body of Christ just as He did creation, for out of the church will appear His Bride. Specifically, and intentionally at this point, are the Spirit and the Bride linked together because the Spirit's assignment is to make her ready for Christ's return; He adorns her.

When Abraham desired to find a wife for his son, his servant was sent to find her from his heritage in another place. The story is found in Genesis 24.

It is symbolic of the Father sending the Dove to find the Bride of Christ in a strange land because we were not born in heaven but become His family through the Spirit's invitation. Once adopted, we are made ready, without spot or wrinkle, for the Bridegroom, who is coming soon.

When the servant met the future wife of Isaac at the well in an unfamiliar country, he marveled at her (v.21). Her name was Rebekah. It signifies the work of the Holy Ghost searching for those of us lost in the world, but notice that she made the searcher marvel; have we ever made God wonder at us?

Above and beyond, Rebekah offered lodging for the man and his camels, which were ten in number (v.25). They were the caravans bringing presents and blessing for the one to become betrothed to Isaac.

As she represents the future Bride of Christ, an interesting point is made here: Do we make room for the Spirit of God when He comes carrying gifts, or do we turn Him away?

Another thing this servant did was, once ushered into the house while dinner was being prepared, he said, "I cannot eat until I have told you about my errand," to which the brother of Rebekah said, "Then speak on" (v.33).

How many times has the Spirit had a message, the mission of God, and we refuse to stop our agenda to listen to what He was saying? We may be cooking, planning an event, working on something strategic for our program, and then the Spirit wants to speak to us. Will we stop what we are doing and give Him our priority?

This man from Abraham's household tells his story of being sent to find a wife for his master's son and finishes with, "But before I had finished speaking in my heart, there was Rebekah" (v.45). It became the second time he was amazed by the future bride's response while on his task. Again, have we made the Spirit of God pause toward us because we have marveled Him or worse, grieved Him?

Finally, the family tried to delay the departure of Rebekah, saying let her remain ten days (v. 55). In the future, this will bear out to coincide with the forthcoming feast schedule: the ten Days of Awe, but the servant replied quickly, "Do not hinder me...that I may go to my master. (v.56)"

Rebekah had to answer for herself. She had to decide if she would go as a bride with the attendant to rendezvous the bridegroom (v. 57-58). Her family could not respond in her place.

Consider the New Testament promise of a Bride and a Bridegroom at the Rapture. How these storylines parallel here, as in the Rapture, the Bride of Christ is asked to go with the Spirit to join the Bridegroom Himself, and it requires a personal reply, not a response of a family name.

Rebekah answered, "I will go" (v.58).

"So, the servant took [her] and departed," (v.61) tells us that at the Rapture, the Bride and the Spirit leave the land they are in, to go to another place to meet the Bridegroom.

It is the Spirit's work to make the Bride ready, and the two are yoked until the time has arrived to come together with Jesus.

And the Spirit and the bride say, "Come!"

Revelation 22:17

15

The Big Reveal of Us

You shall be called by a new name, which the mouth of the Lord will name.

Isaiah 62:2

GOD MAKES THREE CALLS.

The first is when God invites us to salvation, were we receive our identity. Next, He gives a prophetic name over our lives where we sync up with our destiny. But another comes after that where He appoints "our time" when we mature for our part. At the threshold moment, God directs us to enter the main stage and perform our scene.

However, there is a final draw to Himself.

This last decree is a revelation call, showing what we will ultimately become.

As He does this, He sets a unique event into motion, which makes us His own. Theology describes this as consecration, and romantic words paint this as marriage or commitment, but it is when we are set aside for something sacred with God Himself.

A difference is displayed between the Lord speaking our name concerning redemption or destiny and then calling us to Himself. When He speaks our earthly name, He is summoning us to some "thing" (eternal life), just as when He decrees our heavenly name. He also attaches us to a "thing" (a destiny), yet when He calls us to Himself, He is beckoning us to some "One."

He whispers our earthly name in such a way that we realize He is aware of us. We pause in our life path, which was carrying us to death, hell, and the grave, to look up at the One who has insight into who we are. We wonder if questions we have long sought to be answered are about to be so.

Imagine our surprise when Jesus comes to tell us, "You are more than what the natural order can bear; I have another name for you." His prophetic declaration is the disclosure of our spiritual name. We gaze up to view a world never seen before. It is like a curtain that had been closed was suddenly opened to us. Things become quite different from the moment when access to heaven is granted, and we realize they recognize our new name.

> *He who overcomes . . . I will confess his name before My Father and before his angels.*
>
> - Revelation 3:5

Jesus will promote us once we have a name in the spiritual because our book of destiny will be featured in heaven.

> **Our life stories are displayed prominently on the bookshelves of heaven's sacred libraries.**

I intend for mine to turn out to be a best-seller, though, in eternity, copies will not have to be sold. I do, however, set my face like flint that my personal story will be one the saints much desire to read if I have any input into it. I want my life story to be worthy of the read and let this become a battle cry for all of us on the earth as it is in heaven.

What we now understand darkly, heaven comprehends openly; everyone there already understands who we are and into what God destines us to mature. It is a beautiful call, for in it we find our identity and purpose.

Yet something greater is waiting: He wants us for Himself. When He calls us to salvation and then to our destiny, understand more lay ahead. A final drawing to Himself is the end of His upward decrees over us, for then we will be where He is. This last declaration is more than all the others because it completes what Christ intended us to be. We transform into the potential of what we were prophesied to become, even from before the foundation of the world.

When He takes us to Himself, it is very personal.

Peculiar

Now, therefore, if ye will obey my voice indeed, and keep my covenant, then ye shall be a peculiar treasure unto me above all people: for all the earth is mine.

– Exodus 19:5 KJV

GOD CALLS FOR TREASURE.

In this verse, the Lord is telling Moses something unique in all of Scripture, because He was calling a people group, the children of Israel, as His possession. It is not just ownership - which receives such lousy press today, causing people to spew, "You don't own me!" It is something more than that lowly concept. Never is God's idea that abrasive or demanding because His claim over us is based on love, not rights. We shout with vitriol, "No one owns me!" but in this, we concern ourselves with our privileges, yet, when a true embrace comes, our fears melt away. When this happens, our offended liberties disappear. Without the alarm of forfeiting access, God takes us as a holy purchase, for He loves us with a depth no one can explain. Permissions no longer occupy our foremost thoughts because we are assured that we will gain many more allowances than we will lose. Therefore, fear has stopped being our driver, and truth has replaced our rejection; knowing love does not push, it leads. Once we taste this kind of acceptance, no words suffice as we experience intimacy beyond what we thought possible.

It was what God was speaking to Moses about, showing the lawgiver that just as He delivered the people from Egypt's slavery, He would make them His very own possession. I can imagine the revelation Moses was trying to process as the Lord overwhelmed him with visions of salvation, purpose, and ownership. No one could fathom the deep understanding he was receiving.

Though it is difficult to describe, some still attempt to - and do so poorly - causing a misunderstanding of what was honestly being communicated. The King James Version uses this phrase "a peculiar treasure," which, when fully realized, reveals a beauty not commonly received in modern language. It is seen elsewhere when Peter applies it.

> *But ye are a chosen generation, a royal priesthood, an holy nation,* **a peculiar people***; that ye should shew forth the praises of him who hath called you out of darkness into his marvelous light.*
>
> - 1 Peter 2:9 KJV, emphasis added

Often, when we hear this verse in sermons, where the preacher says something like, "And we know we are peculiar people," the congregation laughs. The thought hangs in the air: Christians are crazy.

What an dreadful message taught in the name of making fun of ourselves. We should establish what the Lord is saying here. It would become more precious to us if we do since joyfulness would then be ours instead of a self-deprecating chuckle. We swap joy for giggles, yet our valuable commodity should not be traded so easily if we truly understand its worth. The world thinks we are unhinged because we believe by faith, and since we comprehend how they must view us, this "we-are-crazy-just-deal-with-it" attitude unfortunately becomes our reality.

When we encounter such opposing thoughts, we nod in semi-agreement that we are indeed crazy to trust in a God we cannot see and do things we do not understand. However, this only reinforces the lie that we think in error if we dare see ourselves as extraordinary because the enemy wants us to see ourselves as crazed. It is how unbelievers see us, after all, why should we not consider ourselves in this manner also?

Strictly speaking, this is not the view of our Father in heaven. Once this half-truth takes hold of us, it embeds in our soul and becomes as hard to shake as if a predator were bringing us to the ground. With our heads hung low, we submit to defeat and accept that we must be deranged people.

Absolutely, this is not who we are at all. This mindset is opposed to everything Scripture tells us about those who believe and are saved. We are called the Redeemed, the Remnant, the Bride, and now the "special possession of God."

From the most passionate and contrary position we can muster, we need to cry out, "This is not true, this 'crazy' talk is a lie!"

Try it now, and say with me, "This is untrue, and we are not crazy!" We can do this with a full heart because this is not what peculiar is describing in these passages.

According to today's language, peculiar means strange, odd, or weird, but it had a different meaning a few hundred years ago when the Greek was translated into English. The original description of peculiar is something much more spectacular than crazy, and more honorable. It meant unique, something belonging to only one person as a privilege, distinct from others, or exclusive. It inspires thoughts that we are the rare, uncommon, exceptional, extraordinary, valuable, matchless people of God. We are treasured, cherished, prized, loved, esteemed, and precious. All of us are costly, important, indispensable, invaluable, irreplaceable, adored, and beloved.

What a definition. Let it rewrite our understanding and change how we think of ourselves in the light of this revelation.

What a renewed mind this causes for as believers as we wrestle free of the idea that we are a weird people and start to consider that we are valued instead. We become unparalleled, extraordinary, and precious to the God of the Universe, yet even in humility here in this life, this is what God has spoken of us in His word.

We are made greater than when we began because we have been given a destiny above our earthly beginning

---

Now, we are highly sought after and fought over in the heavenlies. Jesus warred and died (and rose again) for the joy of what He saw we would become: the King's possession.

Brian Louis Perkins

16

The Most Valuable In the World

You shall also be a crown of glory in the hand of the Lord and a royal diadem in the hand of your God.

Isaiah 62:3

During Times of Kings and Queens...

Royalty accumulated gold, silver, and gemstones into their house, calling their collection the peculiar treasure of the king. It meant rare, valuable, and extraordinary jewels, which no one else had, existed in their ensemble as one of a kind pieces becoming the envy of all others.

Precious stones have held a particular lure over people for thousands of years and based upon their ability to reflect light; we set these rare sparklers in categories for the precision of cuts, clarity of stone, and color. The integrity of the object causes the gem to jump in value.

From this assessment, a unique thing happens as the higher a rating is received, the more costly it becomes to obtain. Some become so expensive only monarchs can own them, making their possession a prestige for the owner.

A diamond is something difficult to comprehend at first, because of its unattractiveness; a dirty stone that is hidden deep in the earth. To get near one is challenging, and not always safe, but once discovered and put under the master jeweler's hand, provocative things take place to that smudged little rock. After the facets are formed and polished, the gemstone seizes upon its unique features, adding enormous value when many eyes swoon by its glamorous play with brilliance.

This interactivity with light is why jewels are, well, precious after all. They sparkle and shine, dazzle and flash, and flare and dance. Gems spark a desire for their beauty but let us allow the words "spark" and "sparkle" to take our curiosity for a moment. Both of these terms are linked to lighting, and in them, lay a heavenly truth.

A sparkle reflects direct rays that fall upon its surface, of which it has no defense to be quiet about because the interaction with light causes a riveting spectacle not soon forgotten. It is something that catches our attention.

However, a spark is different, as it is a creation of light, not a response to it, and cannot "spark" without light becoming its main creative ingredient.

When we respond to the light of the Gospel of Christ, it will cause us to sparkle and let the Heavenly Miner know we are interested to play with the light again. When the light creates us, then we have sparked a new creation and become born-again.

But here is a question: Why connect spiritual life with jewels, and more so, those precious metals - gold and silver? Because God created them for a purpose, also, gold is for royalty, and silver is redemption. Jesus was given gold at His birth but sold for silver at His death. Nevertheless, they signify even more epic things than this.

The allegory of gems and rare metals shows us how masterclass Jesus's encounter was with humanity. The Son of

God became the lesson by which we all learn, the depth of knowledge we all seek, and the treasure we all long to have.

Similarly, we are going to be made like Him, for, and that is where the association with jewels comes into play. Because people will be captivated by the handiwork of God wrought in us through our interplay with light, we will become the crowning jewels of God's possession.

Do we catch the eye of the beholder? Are people mesmerized by our shining nature and our dazzling wisdom? They soon will be.

> *Now when they saw the boldness of Peter and John and perceived that they were uneducated and untrained men, they marveled. And they realized that they had been with Jesus.*
>
> *- Acts 4:13*

We are like jewels in this regard, as God's light reflects off of the hard cuts in our lives. These facets were deep chisels in our character. Still, they removed flaws, and now, under the excruciating trials which shaped them, they offer a perfected surface that breathtakingly plays with light. The miracle hand of God has transformed us so we can profoundly radiate with the light from heaven. People will notice with ecstatic wonder at what we have become under the Master Jeweler's artistry.

We know all too well that these hard cuts were devastating. However, excellence has emerged from these actions. From the chastisements to the things we have had to give up, from the separation of things we once loved to the calling we received, we faced difficulties by these deep lacerations into our soul but what they have come to reveal in us now are nothing short of miracles.

Hard surfaces require agonizing cuts before they are ready for display.

Our hard-heartedness and stubborn qualities have to undergo the master jeweler's grind. He must reduce our unwillingness to follow His commands, with our disobedience and rebellions until they are smooth elements, ready for polishing. It takes an abrasive tool to remove hardness, and if we are knit for strength, a heartbreaking abrasion is what God will use. If we are wired for beauty, then He will humble us with trial and test, with whatever instrument is in His toolbox, then He will utilize them to prepare us for an awe-inspiring reveal.

The jeweler not only grinds us smooth if we are hard as diamonds, but He will cast us like gold and silver into serviceable forms if we are soft and pliant. Further, if we have timidity to shine who we were made to be, He makes us firm up our resolve by causing us to walk through the valley of the shadow of death. After this workmanship, we can display our brilliance without flinching.

Most gemstones are sonically cleaned, meaning they are cleansed with sound. It has relevance in a spiritual principle concerning speech. By His word and the sounds, He speaks over us, we, too, are cleansed as a precious thing.

Brian Louis Perkins

> *That he might sanctify and cleanse [the church] with the washing of water by the word*
>
> - Ephesians 5:26 KJV

Also, like gems, we are made valuable under duress with hot pressure and trial. Coal, for example, requires not only pressure, but depth and heat to be transformed into something worthy of a diamond. For formation to occur, it needs to be buried at least 90 feet under the earth's crust while suffering 2000 degrees of heat for the unique conversion to begin. What is exciting about a maceral (pre-organic coal) is that it is defined as an organic, not a mineral. It classifies it as having no crystalline structure, but through this deep burial and heating process, it matures into the glorious rock we all treasure.

> *In this you greatly rejoice, though now for a little while, if need be, you have been grieved by various trials [burial, pressure] that the genuineness of your faith, being much more precious than gold that perishes, though it is tested by fire [heat], may be found to praise,*

> *honor, and glory [treasure] at the revelation of Jesus Christ, whom having not seen you love. Though now you do not see Him, yet believing, you rejoice with joy inexpressible and full of glory, receiving the end of your faith...*
>
> - 1 Peter 1:6-9, added notes mine

The goal is to remove the blemish and produce the pure.

> *Take away the dross from the silver, and it will go to the silversmith for jewelry.*
>
> Proverbs 25:4

> *I counsel you to buy from Me gold refined in the fire, that you may be rich.*
>
> Revelation 3:18

Once the cuts are made, and the corruption removed through cleansing, we have been made precious, useable for honorable purposes as He sets us in place to display His craftsmanship for all to see.

If we do not limit God,
He will make us of limitless beauty.

And at the end of all things, what we will become in our interplay with light is the most marvelous spectacle the world will ever know, far surpassing earthly jewels.

To become a believer in God is the making of us as the most valuable of our kind.

Consider some of the most famous jewels on the earth.[44]

The Hope Diamond is the most well-known in the world, measuring 45.52 carats. A "sister" diamond is The Dresden Green, the largest natural green diamond in the world, weighing 41 carats. The Green is unique; despite the gem's thickness, "it is fairly transparent, a very rare characteristic among diamonds."[45] It also has a clarity rating given only to the upper two percent of naturally colored diamonds in the world.

The Beautiful Call: When God Reveals Our Name

Ronald Winston, son of the famed New York diamond collector, said: "I always hoped that in my lifetime I would be able to witness the Hope Diamond and the Dresden Green on exhibit together."[46]

They were displayed at the same time in the Smithsonian Institution from 2000-2001.

The Graff Pink Diamond is the most flawless in the world. Pinks, in general, are the most scarce to be found of any of the diamonds and even more so any above 5 carats. The Graff Pink Diamond is 23.88 carats. It fell into the top 1 percent of diamonds in the world for clarity, so it was not only the rarest of rare but also of the utmost value. Laurence Graff purchased the original stone for $46 million at a Swiss auction, which at the time was the most expensive in the world. Mr. Graff intended to make it more beautiful by removing its twenty-five flaws with cutting edge technology. At a sizeable risk, he succeeded, and the Graff Pink became internally perfect. Because of this, its current value is too vast to be calculated. [47]

These jewels are now so valuable that it is difficult for any single person to own them. If we were to possess any one of these pieces of finery, not only would financial matters be an issue of the past for us, but we would become world-renowned instantly.

If a king had the Hope Diamond, it would mean he possessed value far above what others owned because his riches were rarer and more highly esteemed than theirs. Therefore, if a monarch gained a "peculiar" treasure, everyone knew what he was holding an exceptional piece of jewelry that no one else could afford.

When the Lord says His people will come to be a peculiar resource, He means that they will be rare and distinguished above all fortunes. When Peter writes that we will be a peculiar people, he is not saying we will be odd, strange, or weird. It is to the contrary that we become the highly prestigious wealth of the King of Kings, that when people consider us, they will know our value is inestimable.

When God calls us to Himself, He will transform us.

He will make us like the Pink Graff Diamond - which was irresistible in its own right. Still, after the master workman removed its internal flaws, it reflects light perfectly. He has made it the most valuable of its kind in the world.

This is a compelling idea God makes for us because it is the heart of the beautiful call.

Brian Louis Perkins

17

The Big Reveal

And they shall call them The Holy People, the Redeemed of the Lord; and you shall be called Sought Out, a City Not Forsaken.

Isaiah 62:12

Godly calls define atmospheres.

Scripture contains the power to change the airspace in which we live. Proclaiming the Word of God causes the rulers of the air to be in confusion and those who issue harassment against us to back off of their "ground." This opens the way for peace to dominant an area with God's presence, and to clear the fog out of the skies about us. With this kind of peace, we are filled with quiet confidence.

Whenever Peter speaks, I pay attention because the Lord invested in this man. He was told things straight from the Lord's lips, and so the revelations he received from the Heavenly Father are recorded. Therefore, when he writes, we should give ear to it. One of the things Peter teaches us is:

> [He] has begotten us again to a living hope through the resurrection of Jesus Christ from the dead, to an inheritance incorruptible and undefiled and that does not fade away, reserved in heaven ... ready to be revealed in the last time...
>
> 1 Peter 1:3-5

Identity is the key to glory

We will be identified, and we will be glorified, shining as the sons and daughters of God that we were ultimately meant to become.

We will be unveiled for everyone to lay their eyes upon, and to be sure God will bring our glorious secret out into the open because it is our final call. When God commands us, we will be transformed into what He envisioned from the beginning.

God is making us the most valuable of our kind in the world

Once the Father removes our flaws by His Son's blood and then reshapes us, He will openly reveal our new kingly station, they will at long last know this secret about those they rejected since He will declare our heavenly name and call us into our time because our destiny is at hand.

The Beautiful Call: When God Reveals Our Name

The world was not worthy of them.

- Hebrews 11:38 NIV

The Word says the entire universe is groaning for us to be set free from death and the grave and put into bodies that will not wear out. It is waiting for our big day.

For the creation waits in eager expectation for the children of God to be revealed.

- Romans 8:19 NIV

David glimpsed briefly at what the weak things of this world would become. Once completed, he called them "excellent." He saw our glorious bodies of immortality; the same ones Paul saw (I Corinthians 15: 35-54).

Paul said our new bodies would have the following characteristics:

- It is a body that pleases God (v. 38)
- It is one of incorruption (v. 42)
- Raised, resurrected (v. 43)

- A glorious body (v.43)
- A powerful body (v. 43)
- A spiritual body (v .43)
- A heavenly body (v. 48)
- A body bearing the image of Christ (v. 49)
- A changed body (v. 51)
- An immortal body (v. 54)

Likewise, Isaiah writes of this type of body in chapter 40 of his book. Notice in verse 26, how God calls out each star by name? He will do this for each one of us as well, and it is a sacred moment because identity, purpose, and timing and our final reveal will be encapsulated in our new spiritual name.

Isaiah describes our new bodies beginning in verse 29 like this:

- A powerful body (v. 29)
- A body of strength (v. 29)
- A body of renewed strength (v. 31)

- A body which can fly as if it had eagles' wings (V. 31)
- A body which never grows tired, nor runs out of energy (v. 31)
- A body which can run and walk without having to stop (v. 31)

Once our revelation happens, those who have opposed us will be ashamed.

God's handiwork has fashioned us marvelously, to form us into the irreplaceable possession of heaven.

Our display will be staged for all the earth to gape at in wonder

Every spirit which harassed, bullied, and harmed us during our time in the fallen world, that broke our will, embarrassed, and frightened us when we were weak, will have a reckoning to come by the relentless strength of our beauty. It will pound the pundits and push them aside. They will be overwhelmed and captivated by what God has done in us, hardly believing their eyes that the people they favored least, have become the Bride of Christ, and the army of the Lamb, controlling undeniable power.

When impenetrability is placed upon us as secured armor, which can never be shaken from our grasp, our enemies will lose heart and never rail against us again.

They will understand we have been infused with grandeur, and that this was the prophetic vision David saw of the excellent ones, and Jesus also saw, for which He laid down His life because of the great joy He witnessed in our revealed names. We will not be shown as weird or strange anymore but displayed as that rare and invaluable treasure everyone desired to become. We have been made into true ourselves.

We will bring prestige to God the Father through Jesus, His Son. Then, remarkably, an uncloaking of extreme power and full-throttled authority of the Holy Spirit descends upon us in the presence of our enemies.

There will never be another revealing like it

We will be presented with Jesus:

Now I saw heaven opened, and behold, a white horse. And He who sat on him was called Faithful and True, and in righteousness, He judges and makes war. His eyes were like a flame of fire, and on His head were many crowns.

He had a name written that no one knew except Himself. He was clothed with a robe dipped in blood, and His name is called The Word of God. And the armies in heaven, clothed in fine linen, white and clean, followed Him on white horses. Now out of His mouth goes a sharp sword, that with it He should strike the nations.

> *And He Himself will rule them with a rod of iron. He Himself treads the winepress of the fierceness and wrath of Almighty God. And He has on His*

robe and on His thigh a name written: KING OF KINGS AND LORD OF LORDS.

- Revelation 19:11-16, emphasis added

Note that Jesus's revealing outshines ours. We will be as glad to be revealed as His people as He will be in showing what He has done in us. The rebellious world will observe the suddenly exquisite Christ. They feared He might one day show Himself to be like this, and then, beyond their greatest anxiety, a million-million jaw-dropping replicas, a billion-billion Christ-like people will instantly be standing with Him.

Imagine them thinking in their way that they were facing just one Champion when without warning, they become surrounded by many. Suddenly throngs of overcoming conquerors encircle their location. And these conquerors are the saints. But these saints are now a bride trained for war, having a taste for victory and triumph.

Your soldiers are willing volunteers on your day of battle; in majestic holiness [holy beauty].

- Psalm 110:3 ISV

Angels who shine and those believers are now revealed as glorified. They will encircle the skies over the camps of the ungodly. The forces of evil will be overshadowed by the breath-taking people of God, and collapse under the weight of their dismay, reluctantly coming to terms with what they never would allow themselves to believe.

They had no idea what they were opposing until too late, for there before them will be those who heard the Beautiful Call and had their names revealed by the Lord. All the demonic plotting and devious scheming will be nakedly exposed before all the world.

> *The kings of the earth set themselves, And the rulers take counsel together, against the Lord and against His Anointed, saying, "Let us break Their bonds in pieces and cast away Their cords from us."*
>
> *- Psalm 2:2-3*

Jehovah God will unleash His strategies, and launch His vast numbers of ready-made righteous battalions, flashing along with the brightness of His coming.

> *And then the lawless one will be revealed, whom the Lord will consume with the breath of His mouth and destroy with the brightness of His coming.*
>
> 2 Thessalonians 2:8

The Lord is guiding us to our Big Reveal

When the generals of this world, at the command of the beast, finally comprehend what they are up against, with shining angels of war bristling everywhere and overwhelming glory bearing down on them from what is intertwined in the Lamb's army, they will run into the rocks saying, "Fall on us!

The Beautiful Call: When God Reveals Our Name

Hide us from the wrath of the Lamb! Who can stand against Him?" (see Rev. 6:16-17).

Therefore, it says that when the leadership of men plan to undo God's "cords" or decrees, the Lord blasts out a laugh, for He knows what is coming.

> *He who sits in the heavens shall laugh; The Lord shall hold them in derision. Then He shall speak to them in His wrath And distress them in His deep displeasure.*
>
> – Psalm 2:4–5

And when He calls us to Himself, we will become like those precious, peculiar treasures.

> *"They shall be Mine," says the Lord of hosts, "On the day that I make them My jewels."*
>
> – Malachi 3:17

We are going to be the crown jewels of God.

For they shall be like the jewels of a crown, Lifted like a banner over His land.

– Zechariah 9:16

The Beautiful Call: When God Reveals Our Name unveils the ultimate destiny of the human race. We must answer Him when He calls, for God will set us in a place above the struggles and worries of this life.

We are God's crowning achievement.

18

If You Hear My Voice:

Since ancient times no one has heard, and no ear has perceived... any God besides you...

　　　　　　　　　　　　　　　　Isaiah 64:4 ISV

About that baby peacock...

Back to the beginning of our story, and we shall revisit the young bird that we left stuck in a tree in a desperate state of affairs. We named him Max because he always pushes everything to its maximum limit. He walks closer to people than any of the other young birds, and he flies higher in the trees, so the name Max is fitting. He is easy to recognize among the chicks because he is bigger and trying to strut his tail feathers as only males do.

Yet today, he is alive and well, doing his "Max" thing because he heard his mother's call and, by listening to her voice, the fledgling found his way out of terror's clutch. The next day, we saw him walking on the ground, living life to the "max."

This baby creature taught us a lesson about harkening to a parent's voice. But God's voice is more excellent, and it is mesmerizing to experience, and through hearing it, we will walk into the light of God's kingdom.

Nothing like it exists anywhere, so if we miss out, regret possesses us because we see what others are discovering. The Lord's call is more beautiful than words can describe. Larger than our circumstance and able to elevate us to our rightful place, this heavenly voice can break our depression. It can guide us out of endangerment and make a way out of no way. We can be called to become what we were made to do, and it is more than death itself, for the beautiful call contains eternal life.

God is calling.

Do you notice its sound?

It is beauty.

It is identity.

It is destiny.

It is timely.

It is time.

It calls our past.

It calls our future.

It calls our now.

It is transforming.

It is life-changing.

It is life.

It is light.

It is the power to alter the atmosphere.

It is the strength to change the world.

It is unpredictable.

It is beautiful.

When we are matured, we, too, can also make an attractive invitation to others. The Spirit reveals us as God's

The Beautiful Call: When God Reveals Our Name

children and the Bride of Christ so that everyone in heaven and earth can see what a wonder God has wrought in us. The big reveal of who we are born to be is a gorgeously, compelling event.

> *Creation eagerly waits for the revealing of the sons of God.*
>
> \- Romans 8:19

All we have to do is watch for Him and give ear to His beautiful call.

> *Therefore, as the Holy Spirit says: "Today if you will hear His voice..."*
>
> \- Hebrews 3:7

To discern the voice of the Lord is the greatest gift any of us could ever have. God speaks now, and He wants to talk to every one of us. Listen to Him whispering your name in a secret place because He desires to have an encounter that will beautify our lives forever.

It is time to hear the Beautiful Call.

Endnotes

1 "H7121 - qara' - Strong's Hebrew Lexicon (NKJV)." Blue Letter Bible. Accessed 2 May, 2020. https://www.blueletterbible.org//lang/lexicon/lexicon.cfm?Strongs=H7121&t=NKJV

2 "H7122 - qara' - Strong's Hebrew Lexicon (NKJV)." Blue Letter Bible. Accessed 2 May, 2020. https://www.blueletterbible.org//lang/lexicon/lexicon.cfm?Strongs=H7122&t=NKJV

3 C. S. Lewis, Mere Christianity (Touchstone, 1996), 155.

4 Mary Drummond, "When God Calls You by Name," XPmedia.com, accessed August 12, 2019, https://www.xpmedia.com/article/19.

5 Bible Plants – Old Dominion University – Myrtle https://ww2.odu.edu/~lmusselm/plant/bible/myrtle.php

6 DeGarmo & Key, "Talk to Me," Heat. It. Up. 1993, Benson, Forefront Communications Group, Inc.

7 "Destiny," https://www.vocabulary.com/dictionary/destiny

8 Robert W. Wall and Eugene Lemcio, The New Testament as Canon: A Reader in Canonical Criticism (London: Bloomsbury, 1992), 130: "Thus I find it unnecessary to engage Williams in the considerable speculation required to make Luke's Peter into Simon bar Jonah. It will be argued, however, that in the larger sense, Peter is Jonah's greater 'son' because for Luke he received the prophetic mantle Jonah once wore."

9 The Story of My Life. Parts I & II by Helen Keller

(1880-1968); Part III from the letters and reports of Anne Mansfield

Sullivan (ca.1867-1936); Edited by John Albert Macy. New York:

Doubleday, Page & Company, 1905.

10 Nicholas Epley, Professor of behavioral science, University of Chicago https://qz.com/935832/why-do-

people-name-their-plants-cars-ships-and-guitars-anthropomorphism-may-actually-signal-social-intelligence/

11 Robert Frost, "The Road Not Taken," Poetry Foundation, accessed August 17, 2019, https://www.poetryfoundation.org/poems/44272/the-road-not- taken.

12 Joseph H. Thayer, Thayer's Greek-English Lexicon of the New Testament, s.v. "ginosko," (Peabody, MA: Hendrickson, 1996).

13 Significance Of The 'Divine Nine' In Ancient Cultures, November 09, 2017, https://www.look4wardstore.com/blogs/news/significance-of-the-divine-nine-in-ancient-cultures

14 https://www.jewishvirtuallibrary.org/roots-of-the-u-s-israel-relationship

15 Edwards, Johnathan. Encyclopaedia Britannica, Shafer, Thomas A. March 18, 2020, https://www.britannica.com/biography/Jonathan-Edwards

16 Ibid

17 Jonathan Edwards, "A Faithful Narrative of the Surprising Work of God," Internet Christian Library

(ICLnet), accessed October 13, 2019, http://www.iclnet.org/pub/resources/text/ipb-e/epl-10/web/edwards- narrative.html.

18 History.com editors, "Great Awakening," History.com, Updated September 20, 2019, https://www.history.com/topics/british-history/great-awakening.

19 J. Edwin Orr, "Prayer brought Revival," accessed August 22, 2019, oChristian.com, http://articles.ochristian.com/article8330.shtml.

20 Ibid.

21 Ibid.

22 Ibid.

23 Richard McNemar, The Kentucky Revival (N.p: Trumpet, 2011), loc. 49 of 2178, Kindle.

24 Ibid., loc. 100 of 2178.

25 Rev. Charles G. Finney, Memoirs of Rev. Charles G. Finney (New York: A. S. Barnes & Co., 1876), 63–65.

26 Richard Klein, "Charles Finney: A Nation's Character Redefined," CBN, Accessed February 4, 2020,

https://www1.cbn.com/charles-finney-nations-character-redefined.

27 Tony Cauchi, "Evan Roberts - 1878-1951," updated November 2007, The Revival Library, http://www.revival-library.org/index.php/pensketches- menu/evangelical-revivalists/roberts-evan.

28 Ibid.

29 Orr, J. Edwin. The Flaming Tongue. Chicago: Moody, 1973.

30 Darrin J. Rodgers, "This Week in AG History – October 7, 1962," Assemblies of God, October 5, 2017, https://news.ag.org/en/Features/This-Week-in-AG- History-October-7-1962.

31 Joseph Smale, The Pentecostal Blessing: Sermons That Prepared Los Angeles for the Azusa Street Revival (Spirit-Empowered) (Springfield, MO: Gospel Publishing House, 2017), loc 75 of 1431, Kindle.

32 "William J. Seymour and the Azusa Street Revival," Assemblies of God, April 4, 1999, https://news.ag.org/en/Features/William-J-Seymour-and-the-Azusa- Street-Revival.

33 The City News Team, "Remembering Billy Graham, God's Ambassador," City News, February 22, 2018, https://www.citynews.sg/2018/02/22/ remembering-billy-graham-gods-ambassador.

34 Pastor Mike Lyle, "Cave Experiences," Sermon preached Crossroad Christian Fellowship, on 11/10/2019.

35 "Lazarus meaning," Abarim Publications, updated August 12, 2019, http://www.abarim-publications.com/Meaning/Lazarus.html.

36 Sea of Galilee « See The Holy Land. https://www.seetheholyland.net/sea-of-galilee-article-israeloutside-jerusalem/

37 Dr. Kevin Zadai, "The Secret Place Episode 1 My visitation with Jesus!" October 15, 2019, https://www.youtube.com/watch?v=be3QzWhzV5s.

38 Kenneth Wuest, Wuest - The New Testament, Matthew 14:28, (Erdman's Publishing Company)

39 Joseph H. Thayer, Thayer's Greek-English Lexicon of the New Testament, s.v. "ei," 2 (Peabody, MA: Hendrickson, 1996).

40 Scott Aniol, "Ordering as Characteristic of the Holy Spirit's Work," Religious Affections Ministries, February 6, 2019, https://religiousaffections.org/articles/articles-on-theology/ordering-as- characteristic-of-the-holy-spirits-work.

41 Wikipedia, s.v. "Cambrian explosion," last modified August 15, 2019, 10:46, https://en.wikipedia.org/wiki/Cambrian_explosion.

42 Jonathan Edwards, "The Holy Spirit: Miscellanies by Jonathan Edwards (1703– 1758)," A Puritan's Mind, accessed August 17, 2019, http://www.apuritansmind.com/puritan-favorites/jonathan-edwards/ miscellaneous-writings/holy-spirit.

43 Camili Mora, "How Many Species Are There on Earth and in the Ocean?" PLOS Biology, August 23, 2011, https://journals.plos.org/plosbiology/article?id=10.1371/journal.pbio.1001127.

44 Bridget Mallon, "13 of the Most Famous Jewels in the World," Veranda, August 21, 2015, https://www.veranda.com/luxury-lifestyle/g1423/most-famous- jewels-in-the-world.

45 Tony Cathaway, "The Dresden Green: The Most Historic Green Diamond," Arpege Diamonds, Naturally Colored Diamond Blog, March 14, 2019, https://blog.arpegediamonds.com/the-dresden-green-the-most-historic- green-diamond.

46 "History of Famous Diamonds," Kissing Solitaire Diamonds, Accessed February 4, 2020, https://kissingsolitairediamonds.com/index.php?route=information/ information&information_id=12.

47 "The Graff Pink Diamond: From Fetching to Flawless," Naturally Colored, accessed February 4, 2020, https://www.naturallycolored.com/famous- diamonds/graff-pink-diamond.

Brian Louis Perkins

About the Author

Brian Perkins is Director of Stormshelter Productions, a non-profit ministry effort for Christian drama. Brian has been producing Christian drama for two decades. He is also a published author of the *GodSpeak* Series, and the seminal *The Passover & the Plaque: A Prayer Guide*, as well as a biblical teacher, faithfully communicating Scripture for over forty years.

Having an ear tuned to the Spirit, stunning revelations come from the overlapping of scientific facts upon in-depth Bible studies with a dash of wordplay. This unique perspective gives readers one aha!-moment after another as they join his journey to discover how, without exception, God is calling us to something greater, and how critical it is to hear His voice.

Desiring to share this message according to the Great Commission, he is releasing these revelatory biblical concepts founded in his love of science that is shaped by the deep authority of Scripture.

Brian lives with his wife, Jamie, in South Florida.

Linq App: Scan the code to visit the Author's website, bio, and bookstore.

Book I - THE BEAUTIFUL CALL: When God Reveals Our Name

Mankind has three questions: Who am I? Why am I here? and, Where am I going? God's beautiful call answers all these and yet He has one call more: He gives us a name.

Names are powerful, carrying identification and authority. But God has a great name above every name. He connects our identity through His beautiful call for He is a name caller. He has a destiny planned for us and is name-calling us into His image.

Names mean something in the spiritual realm. Our first name carries our identity, it is who we are. But God gives us another name, a heavenly one, which holds our destiny; that which we were born to do.

The Beautiful Call: When God Reveals Our Name

When God calls us to Himself, He will transform us. Identity is the key to glory. God is making us into the most valuable of our kind in the world and our display will be staged for all the earth to see. The Lord is guiding us to our Big Reveal.

Available now on Amazon.com.

Book II – THE WHISPER WORD: God Whispers So We Can Roar

Secrets, Strategies, and Power of God's Still Small Voice.

God has a secret weapon the devil cannot defeat; it is His Whisper-Word found in Job 26:14.

God was going to speak in a new way. He was not going to use fearful tones toward us anymore, therefore, God began to whisper. His whispers reveal divine secrets of victory and are personal words from heaven specifically for us. They contain the power to change the world.

Every whispered word from the Lord contains three things: secrets, strategies, and the power to accomplish the given assignment. God can whisper to us in plain sight of our enemy so we can defeat him in our story. A whisper-word from heaven can change a generation.

The Beautiful Call: When God Reveals Our Name

What God whispers in the dark we are to shout on the rooftops. God whispers so we can roar.

Available now on Amazon.com.

Book III –
THE SON-IC HEAVENS:
The Universe Is Telling Us Something

No one found God on the moon when we got there. Our search lies in the desire to hear God's voice. but we do not hear anything with our radio telescopes. No one seems to be speaking to us from the sky.

Yet maybe the heavens aren't so silent after all. They were created by sound, even those who don't believe in a God who speaks, find the Universe full of sound implications. There is more here than meets the eye...or the ear.

In The Sonic Heavens: The Universe Is Trying to Tell Us Something, we will discover that heavens are alive with the sound of the Son of God; they are 'Son'-ic.

The Beautiful Call: When God Reveals Our Name

We will also discover how God made the stars and how He spoke the Universe into existence. Creation testifies of its Creator, and in this, we realize that God is just as delighted to speak with us as He was to make the worlds.

Available soon.

Contact

Linq: Scan the code to visit the Author's website, bio, and bookstore.

Facebook:

GodSpeak Series Page:

fb.me/stormshelterpress

Email:

You can contact Brian at:

stormshelterproductions@gmail.com

Website:

Follow Brian at his Stormshelter Press website:

www.Stormshelterpress.com

www.ingramcontent.com/pod-product-compliance
Lightning Source LLC
LaVergne TN
LVHW041607070426
835507LV00008B/169